About the author

Rachel Bridge is a bestselling author, journalist and public speaker specialising in personal and career development, smart thinking and entrepreneurship. *How to Work for Yourself* is her eighth book, and her other titles include *Already Brilliant: Play to your strengths in work and life*. She is the former Enterprise Editor of the *Sunday Times* and has taken two solo shows to the Edinburgh Fringe Festival. She has an MA degree in Economics from Cambridge University.

Rachel Bridge

How to WORK for Yourself

piatkus

PIATKUS

First published in Great Britain in 2020 by Piatkus

1 3 5 7 9 10 8 6 4 2

A CIP catalogue record for this book
is available from the British Library.

ISBN 978-0-349-42084-4

Typeset in Stone Serif by M Rules
Printed and bound in Great Britain by
Clays Ltd, Elcograf S.p.A

Papers used by Piatkus are from well-managed forests
and other responsible sources.

MIX
Paper from
responsible sources
FSC® C104740

Piatkus
An imprint of
Little, Brown Book Group
Carmelite House
50 Victoria Embankment
London EC4Y 0DZ

An Hachette UK Company
www.hachette.co.uk

www.improvementzone.co.uk

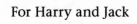
For Harry and Jack

Contents

Introduction

'Life isn't about finding yourself. Life is about creating yourself'

George Bernard Shaw, playwright

Sitting with friends over lunch a while back, I looked around the table and realised that none of them had what might be described as a 'proper' job, with fixed working hours, a regular salary and a career structure. Instead, they all worked for themselves. There was a photographer, a caterer, a business consultant, a writer, an interior designer and a journalist.

A few weeks later I was chatting to a group of sixth-formers after making a speech at their school and discovered that many of them were planning to work for themselves too. Some of them wanted to work with technology, building websites or creating software. Some were hoping to work as garden designers or sports instructors; others wanted to write or design. Many intended to create a way of working that would enable them to travel or live abroad while they continued to develop their careers.

All of them wanted greater control over their working lives

than they felt a traditional salaried job could give them. They didn't want to have to spend hours every day commuting to the same dull office or workplace year after year, being told when to start work and when to have lunch. They didn't like the idea of endlessly seeking approval from a boss in the hope that they might be rewarded with a promotion or pay rise one day. They wanted to be free to work how they chose, developing a career in a way that suited them, instead of plodding through life on someone else's terms.

And then there was me. I have spent more than two thirds of my adult life working for myself, stitching together different skills and interests to create a full-time role. As well as writing books, I make speeches at conferences and other events, I advise small businesses on their communication and marketing strategies, I create content for websites, I write reports and blogs for businesses and I help other people write books of their own.

These different roles perfectly complement and balance each other. When I am writing, I am on my own; when I am making speeches or helping businesses, I am surrounded by other people. One day total silence; the next, the animated buzz of an audience or a meeting in full flow.

I love working like this and I wouldn't want it any other way. It gives me freedom and variety and enables me to meet interesting people.

And all of this got me thinking. With so many people either actively considering or already doing it, working for yourself is clearly no longer a fringe activity – something to do in between jobs, or because you are not able to get the kind of position you want. It is no longer just an alternative sideshow – it has become the main event.

This is borne out by statistics. According to IPSE, the Association of Independent Professionals and the

Self-Employed, there are now more than 2 million people working for themselves in the UK. That's a rise of 43 per cent since 2008. And according to the Office for National Statistics they represent more than 15 per cent of the UK workforce.

I knew that I wanted to explore further.

Why work for yourself now?

The idea of working for yourself has always been appealing, but there are a couple of key reasons why it is becoming increasingly viable right now, no matter what kind of skills you have.

The first reason is technology. Affordable smartphones, laptops, cameras, video conferencing, Google, emails, Wi-Fi and superfast broadband have all made a huge difference when it comes to people working 'together' in different locations. You no longer have to be sitting at the next desk. Technology gives you the ability to work effectively anywhere and yet still stay connected to colleagues and customers.

The second reason is availability of work. Working for yourself makes so much sense right now because businesses and individuals are more willing to hire freelancers and independent contractors to do work that might have traditionally been done by an employee. That means there is a rapidly growing amount of work available; and depending on the skills required, it can be surprisingly well paid.

Businesses are choosing to hire workers this way because it gives them access to skills they don't have in-house, something that is becoming more and more important as the expertise required to run their business successfully becomes more highly specialised. Even if they wanted to, many firms would find it impossible to employ people who could provide all the skills they need, particularly in fast-changing areas such as technology, digital, marketing and IT.

Hiring workers on a freelance or self-employed basis also means that only specific skills need to be paid for, and only when they are needed, which saves on costs. And businesses can get the relevant people on board really quickly, giving them far greater flexibility to react to sudden changes in their markets. It takes time to find and hire a permanent employee, but a self-employed freelancer or contractor can often start work on a project straight away. Businesses also know they are going to be highly motivated to do a good job, because otherwise they won't last long working for themselves.

Chris Bryce, chief executive of IPSE, says: 'We are seeing increasing use of highly skilled self-employed people, particularly in larger projects. Businesses are recognising that a freelancer has an incentive to deliver and be good which might be lacking in some permanent employees. Freelancers are increasingly starting to get the good, interesting work because they are regarded as a "will deliver, high talent" sector.'

A survey by the freelancing platform Upwork found that 59 per cent of hiring managers in the US already use freelancers and other temporary talent to supplement the skills and availability of their employed workforce, with most believing that this trend will significantly grow over the next decade. It is clear that this is happening in the UK too.

Indeed, large corporate businesses are becoming so concerned about losing their top-quality consultants to self-employment that they are creating schemes that will enable former employees to work for them on a freelance basis. The big accountancy firm PWC has created a Flexible Talent Network to enable qualified accountants to work flexibly for them on an ongoing basis – perhaps for only part of the year, or only during school term time, or for reduced hours or whatever suits them.

At the same time, individuals are also becoming more comfortable with the idea of paying other people to do tasks which they don't have the time or ability to do themselves, whether that's creating a website or walking their dog. The past decade has seen a surge in demand for personal and domestic services that people pay for by the hour. This has opened up all kinds of opportunities for people to work for themselves by providing these services to their local community and beyond.

Defining this way of working

A quick word about terminology. I've used 'working for yourself' throughout this book as an umbrella term to describe the many strands of working independently, such as freelance, self-employed, independent contractor and solo business, a phrase popular in the US which describes people who run businesses that will only ever employ themselves.

Now, I know that the phrase 'working for yourself' is not perfect. After all, unless you are Banksy, you are not working for yourself in the sense that you can simply beaver away at your own personal projects and hope that they will somehow bring in an income. In reality, most people who are working for themselves are actually doing work for clients, who have either commissioned or hired them to carry out a specific task.

However, I've chosen to use 'working for yourself' as it's the best we have right now, and because it reflects the fact that working this way is about putting you in control – of your working hours, your working environment, the kind of work you choose to take on and how much of it you decide to do. By providing your services in a way that you are comfortable with, you are in control of the process and you are doing it on your own terms, according to your own rules. You get to decide if you want to take on a piece of work, and then, depending on the type of service you offer, you may also get to choose when you do it, how you do it, where you do it and how long you take to complete it.

How this book can help you

Working for yourself can be an incredibly rewarding way of making a living, giving you more freedom, control, fun, satisfaction and income than you could have imagined. But if you have never done it before, it can be difficult to know where to start, how to get established and what pitfalls to look out for along the way.

This book is a step-by-step guide, showing you how to do it in an effective, fulfilling and rewarding way. Drawing on my own extensive experiences and those of many others who already work for themselves, it contains practical advice and information, real-life examples and essential top tips to help you make a successful transition to working for yourself. You'll learn how to decide if this is the right path for you, how to get started, the key issues you need to think about and how to overcome obstacles – not just from a practical point of view, but from a personal, financial and emotional perspective too.

So whether you are currently in a salaried job and exploring the idea of going it alone, about to take your first step into the workplace after school or university, have just been made redundant or are already working for yourself but need help and guidance on how to do it better, this is the book for you.

Now let's get started.

Chapter 1

Why do you want to work for yourself?

'To live is the rarest thing in the world. Most people just exist'

Oscar Wilde, playwright

There are lots of potential benefits to working for yourself, but some of them are going to be more important to you personally than others, so it makes sense to identify from the outset which of them would make a real difference to your life.

Let's take a look at some of these now, so you can see clearly what you are aiming for and the rewards you will gain by making the switch.

You can do something you love

Abby Gregory spent six years working in an office for a travel company, ending up as product manager, but she always dreamed of being able to work with animals, having grown up around horses and looked after rescue dogs. So when she was made redundant, she seized the chance to create her own job and became a dog walker in her home town of Cheltenham and the surrounding area.

Abby now walks thirty dogs a week and makes more money than she did from her salaried job. She says: 'I tried working in an office because I thought I needed to knuckle down and get a proper job. But the whole time I was there I wished I was outdoors working with animals. It is hard work and I do long hours, often walking 20 kilometres a day, but I love it. I couldn't do a nine-to-five job working for somebody else now.'

You can decide when you work

Much of the work done by freelancers and self-employed people is output-based and for an agreed set fee, meaning that it doesn't matter how or when you do it, as long as the end result is good. If you are writing a piece of software for someone or making them a wedding cake, they don't care how long it took you, or when you actually did the work – they just want to know that the finished software or cake is fantastic. So if you take on these kinds of projects as a self-employed worker, you have an immense amount of freedom to design your working day exactly as you want it. You may prefer to start work early in the morning, for example, or work late into the night. You may choose to fit your working hours around the needs of other family members or do three extra-long days and take the rest of the week off. However you choose to shape your working hours, it can be a hugely refreshing change from a salaried job that requires you to be at work at a particular time each day and stay for a certain number of hours, regardless of what needs doing.

Indeed, a recent survey of freelance workers by price comparison website Moneysupermarket.com found that 59.6 per cent regarded the flexibility of working hours as the single biggest benefit of working for yourself.

Damon Jones earns a good daily rate working for himself as an interim executive in the private equity industry, going into private equity-backed firms and helping them with specific projects to grow their businesses. There is a lot of demand for his services and he could easily do what most other interim executives do and sign up to work every working day of the year. But instead Damon has chosen to make the most of the freedom that working for himself offers. So he works just ninety days a year, spending the rest of the time doing all the other things he loves, such as running his own property-development business or helping out with the caravan park that his wife set up on their farm in Suffolk.

Working this way also means that Damon is able to spend large amounts of time at his other home in southern Spain, typically spending three months there each winter. He has created a home office out there which is an exact copy of his home office in the UK, with linked computers, making it easy for him to stay on top of work commitments if he needs to.

Damon clearly enjoys being able to live and work this way. He says: 'I could work 220 days in the public sector earning really good money every year, churning the work out like a sausage machine. But it would drive me absolutely insane. I do this because I absolutely love doing it. For me it is about lifestyle. I turned down two permanent roles last year because I didn't want them. I have got one of the best jobs in the world.'

Decide where you work

If you can supply your own tools or equipment – whether that is a laptop, a camera or a pair of hairdressing scissors – and work on a project on your own, then you can locate yourself pretty much anywhere you want, even overseas.

That's what Cass Helstrip did. After many years of working in a salaried job as a public-relations consultant for the travel industry, she decided to work for herself at the age of 31. She started out based in a co-working space in London, but soon realised that she could just as easily work abroad. So she began working overseas for a few weeks at a time, taking her laptop with her to work in places such as France, Thailand and the US.

Eventually, at the age of 37, she moved to Ibiza for a year, renting an apartment there to live and work in, and flying back for one week every month for meetings with journalists and clients. She would stay in a friend's spare room for the week she was back in London.

She says: 'It was an amazing experience and there were so many cheap flights from Ibiza to London that I could be back within a few hours whenever I needed to. I used to work on the balcony of my apartment which overlooked the swimming pool, which I absolutely loved.'

Cass's clients were very happy with the arrangement too, many of them going out to stay with her. She even picked up some new clients in Ibiza.

There was just one thing she had to be aware of. She says: 'I did have to be careful with social media. While my clients completely trusted my commitment, they didn't much like me posting photos of the beach while they were stuck in an office.'

You can vary the work you do

When you work for one employer in one job it is easy to get stuck in a rut doing the same kind of work, over and over again, because of the rigid expectation and structure around the work you do each day. If you work in the marketing department of a company, it would be unthinkable for you to suddenly decide that you'd like to join the design team for a week or be part of the sales team for a few days. You may be able to deviate from your job description occasionally, perhaps by suggesting an exploratory side project, but not by far, and not for long, because you would also need to be doing your own clearly defined job. Even if you are delivering a tangible benefit to the business performing one of these other roles, you are likely to find yourself stepping on someone else's toes or encroaching on someone else's territory and will be quickly reined back in.

When you work for yourself, however, you have much more freedom to take on different kinds of work in a variety of areas. Provided you have the relevant skills, you can do marketing one week, writing the next and designing the week after. Instead of enduring the monotony of working on the same thing with the same people week in, week out, you can benefit from the freshness that comes from a range of projects requiring different skills. This can be personally enriching, and it can give you a wider perspective of your industry.

As long as you are not working for a direct competitor, your clients don't need to know what other work you are doing, who you are doing it for or how much of it there is. Which means that you can develop a whole portfolio of different types of roles, and you will never get bored.

You can change the nature of your relationships with people you work for

When you are in a salaried job your boss has all the power: they get to decide what you do and how you do it; and if you get it wrong, they can fire you. But working for yourself creates a completely different kind of dynamic. That's because instead of being employed by only one person who can decide that they don't want you to work for them anymore, you can work for lots of different people, all at the same time. That lessens your dependence on any one employer, and takes away their ability to decide your fate – because if you don't like the deal that's being presented, or you hate the working relationship on offer, you can simply walk away and get other work elsewhere. This turns the relationship between you and the people you are doing work for into a much more equal partnership.

You can explore new areas of work in a low-risk way

When you are in a salaried position it can be hard to move into a new area without changing jobs, because if you are any good at what you do, your boss is likely to want you to keep on doing it, again and again. In addition, changing jobs involves major upheaval and can be a high-risk strategy if you have no real idea whether you are going to like the new role any better than the one you are giving up. When you work for yourself, however, you can easily try out new areas in a short-term, low-risk way to see if you like them. Getting some work creating a logo or organising an event does not commit you to being a logo designer or event organiser for the next five years; you merely have to do it until the project you have taken on is complete. If you discover that you hate it, you can simply avoid that kind of work in future.

You can create a more pleasant working environment

For me this is easily the greatest joy of working for myself. No more shivering in offices because the air conditioning is turned up too high or wondering what the weather is like outside because there are no windows to look out of. At home I can turn the heating up as high as I want, whenever I want. And I can put my desk by the window, so that on sunny days I get a nice view and fresh air. Best of all, unless I am going to a meeting, I can wear what I want and no one cares – no more uncomfortable jackets and high heels for me. Bliss.

You can pursue your own projects while still earning a living

Phil Lowe is a successful leadership coach who works with senior business executives to help them become more effective at work. He also writes and directs films. His short film *The Driving Seat* was shown at 40 festivals worldwide and won six awards, including Best Comedy Film at the Isle of Man festival.

At the moment, Phil doesn't make much money from his film projects. If he was in a full-time job he would have to squeeze his film work into evenings and weekends. But because he works for himself, he is able to make time for this and his coaching work. He splits his week roughly equally between his two roles, blocking out time in his diary for film projects and then fitting his more lucrative coaching work around it.

Phil says: 'One side supports the other side. My daily rate as a corporate coach is higher than if I was an employee, so I don't have to do it every day, and I don't have a boss to justify my time to. I also have the freedom to say no to work if I choose to.'

He adds: 'I have writer friends who work full-time and can only write in the evenings and I have to be careful not to appear too smug about all the time that I have in which to write.'

As a result, Phil is also much happier. He says: 'If I couldn't coach ever again I would certainly miss it, but if I couldn't write ever again it would feel like part of me being cut off.'

You can make more money

There is a widely held belief that working for yourself will mean having to make do with a lower income. But it's just not true. Many of the people I know who work for themselves make far more money now than they ever did in a salaried job.

They are not necessarily working harder, they are just working smarter. Look at the time you waste in a typical job: all those hours spent getting to and from work, chatting to colleagues at the water cooler and wandering around the shops in your lunch hour. All of that wasted time can be put to much better use when you are working for yourself, allowing you to take on multiple projects, work more productively and generally get a lot more done.

You can step away from the petty squabbles of workplace life

Being an employee rarely means simply turning up for work and getting on with your job – there is all the other stuff you have to get involved in too, from time-consuming appraisals and assessments to team-building exercises.

But when you work for yourself you are judged solely on the quality of the work you do, rather than on your ability to win at office politics. You don't have to sit through endless strategy meetings, you don't have to get involved in performance reviews and you don't have to sit next to someone you cannot stand, every day. You can simply get on with your job.

TOP TIP

Get in touch with anyone you know who already works for themselves and ask if you can have a chat with them about why they have chosen to work this way. Ask them to tell you honestly what they particularly like and dislike about the arrangement and what advice they would give you. By talking to someone you know personally, you should come away with some real insights into how it works in practice.

Chapter 2

Do you have the personal skills to go it alone?

'Start where you are. Use what you have. Do what you can'

Arthur Ashe, tennis player

Working for yourself is not just about doing work in a different way – it entails a whole shift in mindset which, depending on your attitude and approach, can either be exciting and liberating or scary and daunting. So before we go any further, let's look at whether working for yourself is going to be the right choice for you, and whether your own personality traits would make this a good or bad option for you.

There are a number of traits you will either need to have already or to develop if you are to make a success of working for yourself. Here are some of the most important ones:

Self-motivation

When you are in a salaried job you can probably cruise through a day, a week or even several months without achieving very much, and you will still get paid at the end of the month. Not so when you are working for yourself. Nothing will happen without you driving it. This means that you have to be able to motivate yourself both to pitch for work and to do the work on time, every time, because no one else is going to do it for you.

Tenacity

It can be difficult finding work, particularly when you are starting out. You are trying to create something out of nothing, and it is not going to happen overnight. And it can be just as hard keeping the work coming in. You may have to deal with a lot of rejections before you get a yes, and then deal with more rejections before you get your next yes. You must be able to bounce back if you don't land work you had hoped to get or a project you were working on ends sooner than expected.

Ability to stay calm under pressure

When you work for yourself, regardless of the kind of work you are doing, you are unlikely to have the kind of support or back-up resources that you would have in a job. That means the buck pretty much stops with you – if something goes wrong, you need to be able to stay calm and clear-headed and fix it on your own, without collapsing in a heap.

Julia Maddox works for herself as a caterer, having decided to go it alone after working in a restaurant for a few years. She typically caters for parties, anniversaries and other special occasions.

Over the years, she has had to be extremely resourceful and

learn how to deal with problems herself as they arise. Once, she was doing the catering for a reception at a grand house in the countryside. The client wanted to impress his American guests by serving Bloody Mary cocktails, but as the party got under way Julia discovered that he had not ordered enough tomato juice.

She says: 'The house was really remote, so there wasn't enough time to go and buy more, but I knew that the client would have been really upset if I'd told him. In desperation, I searched in the kitchen cupboard and found some tinned tomatoes, whisked them up in the blender with some crushed ice and Worcestershire sauce and used that instead, adding a celery stick as a garnish. No one was any the wiser, and the guests loved it so much that some of them even asked for the recipe.'

Julia has now developed her own method of dealing with an unexpected crisis. She says: 'I always tell staff who help me at events, don't ever panic until I panic. Meanwhile I take a very deep breath and count to ten in my head. It really does work.'

Good organisational skills

This is vital, not just to stay on top of your work, but to stay on top of your personal life too. When you work for yourself you will find that a ridiculous amount of your time is taken up with admin that keeps the whole show on the road – pitches, proposals, invoices, contracts, tax returns, VAT returns, arranging meetings, building up a database of contacts, marketing activity. All of this needs to be managed and kept under control, otherwise it will quickly overwhelm you.

But you will need to get organised on a personal basis too, now that you no longer have access to the services you may have taken for granted in a salaried job, such as a PA to update your diary and remind you to attend meetings, access to an IT expert to fix your computer, freely available stationery, the use of a printer permanently stocked up with ink and paper and even regular flu jabs arranged by the firm. You are on your own now, so seek out your inner organised elf, make lists, keep track of useful information and stay in control. You may hate having to do all this stuff, but it is a fundamental part of working for yourself. Each is impossible without the other.

Self-reliance

When you work for yourself you need to be able to work independently on a project without constant motivation and guidance. Clients are paying you for your expertise, so once they have given you a piece of work, they expect you to know what you are doing and to get on with it without having to hold your hand while you are doing it.

If you are unsure about how to do something when working for an employer, it's likely that there will always be someone around you can ask for advice. When you work for yourself, however, if a decision needs to be made, then you are the one who will need to make it.

Simon Foster works as a project manager on IT projects, such as helping companies move their IT systems on to a new platform. He works from home, managing teams of three or four people, and occasionally a lot more, remotely. 'For most of the jobs I do, I am just left to my own devices,' says Simon. 'I have someone I report to, who can help me if I need it, but generally I am just left alone to get on with it. I like being able to work like that.'

Simon uses technology to manage his teams and get projects completed. He explains: 'I manage my teams by getting everyone involved to use chat windows on their computer screens. This means that I can see all the conversations that are going on and it gives me a good oversight and visibility of everything that is happening and what the issues are. My teams all talk to each other in the chat windows and I can jump in whenever I need to to deal with issues as they arise. At the moment I am managing several projects, so I have different chat windows on, and this technology allows me to manage multiple projects at the same time across multiple hours and sometimes across multiple time zones.'

Having to be self-reliant suits Simon's personality: 'I like solving problems and trying to think of ways to make things happen.'

Reliability

Being reliable is the single most effective way to stand out from the crowd and ensure that you are given the work rather than someone else. If you want to work for yourself you must be able to deliver what you said you would, when you said you would, otherwise clients won't bother to use you again. They need to be able to trust you to deliver. That means showing up on time, hitting deadlines and doing that each time, every time. The very best compliment I have ever been given is, simply: 'She gets the job done.'

Flexibility

A very useful trait for working for yourself is the ability to be adaptable and flexible. A client might change their mind about the direction of a project or your role within it midway through, or they could even ditch it altogether. They might want you to drop everything to help them get a project off the ground, and then change their mind a week later. This can be infuriating, but you need to be flexible and adaptable enough to handle this sort of unpredictability. Work can often arrive out of the blue and at short notice, but the good news is that if you are able to operate like this in an unflappable way and still deliver good work, then clients will put you on speed dial and the work will flow in.

Willingness to keep learning

You may have some fantastic skills to offer clients, but if they are not what your clients want or need right now, then you will need to learn new ones. That might mean retraining, getting additional qualifications or experience or learning how to use new equipment.

Ability to park your ego

Even if you always secretly felt that job titles were rather silly and pointless when you were in a job, it can feel surprisingly odd when you no longer have one. When I left my job at the *Sunday Times*, I felt strangely disorientated when I suddenly realised that I was no longer Rachel Bridge, Enterprise Editor of the *Sunday Times*; instead I was now just plain Rachel Bridge, editor of nothing from nowhere. Initially it can be difficult to get used to that, particularly when you ring someone in an office and the receptionist asks you where you are calling from and you don't know what to say. You can of course give yourself a new title, perhaps describing yourself as the founder or managing director of your own newly created business, but the sooner you can make the mental adjustment and accept that now you are just plain you, the better.

Willingness to create your own path

Choosing to work for yourself means that you may hit life's milestones in the wrong order, in a different way or even bypass them altogether. Without an employment contract paying a regular monthly salary, you may find it harder to get a mortgage, for example. But equally, you may find that your ability to work from anywhere means that you can live somewhere really cheaply while you save every penny you earn, so that eventually you can buy somewhere with a substantial deposit or even outright, avoiding the need for a mortgage altogether.

A sense of adventure

Working for yourself means stepping into the unknown, so you need to be willing and able to embrace the unpredictable and the unforeseeable. This is not the career path for someone who gets easily stressed, panicky or anxious. In fact, it can be a roller-coaster ride. Sometimes it will feel easy and the best job in the world, as interesting, well-paid work flows in, while at other times it will feel horrible when the work dries up and you have to chase everyone for money they owe you. Your income will be erratic, your work flow will be irregular, and although there are things you can do to manage this – as you will see later in the book – you have to be able to accept that volatility without feeling overwhelmed every time there is a dip in the amount of work and money coming in.

If you can approach it with a sense of optimism and excitement, the more successfully you will sail through it – and the more likely that your enthusiasm will be apparent to clients, making them want to give you work.

TOP TIP

Ask three friends or work colleagues to describe your best personal qualities in three words. Do any of these relate to qualities you will need to work for yourself? Do any of them say the complete opposite? Building up an idea of your strengths will be very useful in helping you decide whether this is the route for you.

Chapter 3

Identify and sharpen your work skills

'Pleasure in the job puts perfection in the work'

Aristotle, philosopher

Now that you have identified the personal skills required to work for yourself, you need to think about the kind of work skills you have and how you might be able to use them to earn money.

Start with what you know

Look at the experience and skills you have already gained through studying, or by working for someone else, and think about how you might be able to use – or adapt – them to create a service you can offer clients. You may be able to do exactly the same kind of work as before, or you may need to tweak or only use some elements of it. Either way, it makes a lot of sense to use what you can already do as a base. You can always add more knowledge and skills as you go along.

Start by analysing the kind of work you have done in the past. Did it involve writing, or researching, or creating, or analysing? Were you managing or organising? Did you work with words, pictures or numbers? The more skills you can identify, the more flexible you can be about the type of work you take on.

Focus on an area of speciality

While you may be able to make a living offering a basic level of skills in your chosen area, the real money is in creating a niche for yourself. That's because businesses are increasingly looking for freelancers or contractors who specialise, and they are prepared to pay good money for them. Instead of simply looking to hire a good software developer, for example, they may want someone who can offer specific expertise in data science, cyber security or blockchain technology, and who can use the latest online tools and applications associated with them. An ability to speak another language, or several, is another highly prized skill. Not only are you likely to be paid more for this expertise, you will find yourself with a regular stream of work.

Sarah Kane works for herself as a freelance translator, copy-editor and proofreader specialising in art history, translating books and exhibition catalogues from Italian, German and French into English for prestigious museums and publishers around the world. This rare combination of skills she is able to offer means that she is never short of work.

Sarah decided to establish herself in this area after working for a publishing house in London and realising that she wanted to find a way of combining the subjects she had studied, which included a BA in foreign languages and literature, an MA degree in art history and a diploma in translating.

She says: 'I was very keen to use the subjects that I had studied and having done quite a lot of editing while working for the publishing house, I knew I was good at it. It felt as though it would have been a waste to spend all those years studying and not to do anything with it. I also knew it was something that interested me and that I would enjoy. I go to art exhibitions and museums in my spare time, so my working life and interests align. Sometimes the books I am working on are literally bang in the middle of the subject areas that I studied. I feel very lucky.'

Fill in the gaps

If you are missing some of the skills you need to be able to offer a particular service, you will need to acquire them, or else clients will hire someone else who already has them. Jobs listed on freelance job sites can provide a good idea of the skills clients expect freelancers to have in order to be able to do a specific project. A job advertised on Upwork (www. upwork.com) for a web developer, for example, requires the successful applicant to be familiar with CSS3, HTML5, JavaScript, VueJS and Yii.

You may be able to take an online course to acquire the skills you lack. Online e-learning course providers in the UK have substantially expanded both in number and in the kind of courses they offer in the past few years. LinkedIn Learning (www.linkedin.com/learning), for example, offers hundreds of online courses suitable for professional freelancers, designed to enable you to become a graphic designer, a video editor, a search engine optimisation (SEO) expert or a data scientist, among other things. The courses take the form of videos and they are divided into modules, so you can watch them in segments.

Other online e-learning providers include Udemy (www.udemy.com), PluralSight (www.pluralsight.com), SkillShare (www.skillshare.com) and Udacity (www.udacity.com).

Offer complementary skills

Wherever possible, try to offer clients a complete service, so reducing the need for them to bring in other self-employed workers to finish a project. Being able to create a website and also to actively promote it on the Internet using SEO are two complementary skills to be able to offer, for example. The more you can corner a particular area of the market and avoid a client having to hire someone else to do the bits that you can't, the better.

Walk the talk

Whenever possible, demonstrate the skills you are offering clients in your own life. If you are setting yourself up as a social-media expert, say, make sure your own personal social-media channels look amazing and are already doing everything you are claiming you can do for your client. If you can only muster twenty-seven followers and a history of nine tweets, they are not going to be very impressed.

Rachel Mounter is a great example of how to walk the talk. Today, she thinks nothing of running marathons and half marathons, but when she first graduated from university, she was 30kg overweight and deeply unhappy. She tried to lose weight, but struggled to make much progress until she got a personal trainer, who introduced her to different kinds of exercise and enabled her to get back in shape.

Rachel was so inspired by the difference a personal trainer could make that when she was made redundant from her office job as a PA she decided to become one herself. She now uses her experience to motivate her clients to lose weight and get fit.

She says: 'I lost 30kg myself, so I understand where people are coming from. I always hated exercise, but when I got a personal trainer, he introduced me to different ways of training and I discovered that it doesn't have to be boring – it can be fun. A lot of personal trainers have always been fit, so they don't understand how hard it can be to lose weight. But I am not perfect, which I think is why people like me. I am real. I still have issues with my weight; I am not skinny and I still like to eat chocolate and crisps and drink alcohol. I tell my clients that it is not about having a six-pack; it is about having a healthy, happy body and lifestyle.'

To inspire her clients further, Rachel also posts 'before' and 'after' pictures of her dramatic weight loss on her website and social-media pages, and shares news about races she is taking part in: 'I have never been good at talking about myself and I hate putting pictures of myself online, but I have had to get over that because it does help people connect with me and realise that maybe I can help them. I feel so privileged to be able to do this and find it extremely rewarding.'

Embrace technology

No matter what kind of work you are looking to do, you will be able to do it better if you have a good grasp of technology, whether that is using an app to schedule meetings, making a Skype call, working on shared digital documents or uploading a photo on to your client's online database. If a client asks you to use a piece of technology that you are not familiar with, don't shriek in horror – simply ask if someone from their IT team could talk you through it, so that you understand how it works. Whatever industry you are in, the more tech savvy you are, and the more confident you are about using digital online tools, the more attractive you will be to a prospective client.

TOP TIP

IPSE, the organisation which represents the self-employed, has a learning hub on its website (www.ipse.org.uk) called the IPSE Academy which offers a range of courses for people who work for themselves, including accounting and finance, business skills and legal basics. Check it out to identify areas in which you can expand or improve your skills.

Chapter 4

What kind of work are you going to do?

'Whatever you are, be a good one'

Abraham Lincoln, American president

These days, all kinds of work can be done by someone who works for themselves, and the range is expanding as more and more people, organisations and industries see the benefits of hiring people to work this way.

Having identified both your personal skills and professional areas of expertise, it's now time to start thinking about the kind of work you would most like to do. Here are some examples of the types of self-employed work that are currently most in demand – take a look and see which of them spark your interest and excitement:

Events organiser

If you love throwing parties and organising big family events, and you are really organised in your own life, then you could work for yourself organising other people's special occasions.

Wedding planners in particular are increasingly in demand, as people's expectations of their big day – and the amount they are prepared to spend on it – soar.

Digital technology expert

Cloud computing, blockchain technology, machine learning, augmented reality, robotics, Internet of Things – there is extensive demand for people who really know their stuff in these areas, whether that be helping a business to move its data storage into the cloud or helping them incorporate artificial intelligence into their systems. With these technologies changing so quickly there will be no shortage of businesses keen to find freelancers who can use the latest tools and applications with ease.

Virtual PA

Many small start-up businesses would love to have a personal assistant (PA) to help organise their admin, but can't afford to pay for a full-time one – which is where you might come in. A virtual PA offers many of the same services as a traditional one – typing, transcribing, writing letters, organising diaries and work schedules, for example – but they work remotely, staying in contact via email and phone. This is a win-win: the client has fewer overheads, while the PA can work for several people at once.

Health and beauty practitioner

As our lives get busier, there is a growing demand for services which customers can enjoy at home, rather than having to spend time getting to a salon or wellness centre. Mobile hair-dressers, make-up artists and nail technicians are all popular services, as well as people who can offer reiki, reflexology, hypnotherapy and nutritional advice.

Writer or editor

Making a living solely as a freelance journalist has become increasingly difficult as newspapers and magazines cut their payment rates or even close in the face of intense competition from online publications. However, businesses and other organisations also have an ongoing need for well-written pieces for their websites, blogs, newsletters, reports, marketing campaigns and so on. You obviously need to be good at writing, but you must also be good at getting the right tone, as well as delivering the piece on time to the prescribed length. Editing might involve commissioning and co-ordinating writing produced by others and then shaping these pieces to fit the required length and style.

Craftsperson

Using traditional crafts to make interesting and unusual handmade products – perhaps combined with teaching others how to do this for themselves – has become hugely popular in recent years and offers many potential ways to work for yourself. Websites such as Etsy.com and Notonthehighstreet.com offer highly popular online marketplaces where you can sell the things you make. If you can knit or crochet, make clay pots or weave a rug, then you may be able to earn a living this way.

Data analytics expert

This field is expanding fast as businesses try to make sense of all the data that their technology applications are producing. People who know about data science and how to use the software associated with it are much in demand.

Graphic designer

If you have a flair for creative design, you are always going to be in demand from businesses who need freelancers to design logos, websites and marketing materials for them and who know how to use the latest professional design software.

Social-media marketer

As more businesses start to engage with their customers online via social media, they need freelancers with the right skills and expertise to run and manage their social-media accounts on Twitter, Instagram, Facebook and others. An extension to this role is content strategy, which involves developing, managing and co-ordinating content across several platforms and channels, including social media and other forms of online presence.

Plumber, electrician or other tradesperson

If you have the relevant skills and qualifications or are prepared to gain them, there will always be a demand for people who know how to fix a boiler, rewire a house or tile a bathroom.

Business consultant

Consultancy is an all-purpose word covering a range of different situations, but if you have hands-on experience of a particular industry and how it works, then businesses may be interested in hiring your services by the day to advise and guide them on their strategy.

Tutor

Becoming a tutor has long been a source of income for freelancers and the potential for work has considerably opened up in recent years, as tuition moves online. Tutors who can conduct lessons over the Internet are increasingly in demand to help everyone from time-strapped students needing to pass critical exams to providing lessons for home-schooled children. This also means that tutors are no longer restricted to providing tuition in their local area or as far as they are willing to travel, and can do so from anywhere that has a good broadband connection.

Marketing and PR consultant

If you have good communication skills and enjoy being able to explain potentially complex products, services and ideas in an easy-to-understand way, then marketing and PR can provide lots of opportunities for you to earn a living. Both these roles are essentially all about getting a message across, whether in a press release or phone call to journalists, or through a marketing campaign to consumers. Because they are often centred around specific events, such as the launch of a new product, you can often work on a project basis, providing your skills and expertise to businesses that could not afford to hire someone on a full-time basis.

Translator

This is another area in which there is plenty of competition, not least from increasingly sophisticated computer software, but if you can find yourself a niche – for example, translating highly technical medical journals or scientific papers – you will improve your chances of getting work.

Caterer

If you can rustle up a dinner party for twelve at short notice or bake a show-stopping birthday cake, there are many ways you could use your cooking and baking skills to work for yourself. You might choose to specialise in catering for large events or small dinner parties, or you might decide to focus on a particular type of cooking such as vegan, gluten-free or a distinctive regional cuisine.

Cyber-security specialist

As more and more of our lives are conducted online and we become comfortable with doing financial transactions via the

Internet and storing our data in the cloud, the threat posed by cybercriminals becomes ever more real, particularly as their tactics become more sophisticated. As a result, there is a growing demand for freelancers who can offer their skills in this area.

Video editor

Anyone who has a teenager at home will know that videos make up a large proportion of the content viewed on the Internet these days. All those memes, gifs and YouTube clips don't just make themselves. Video is increasingly being used as a marketing tool by businesses too, as well as for enter- tainment, and freelancers with skills in this area will be in demand for some time to come.

Accountant

Becoming an accountant takes a lot longer than learning how to edit a video, but if you happen to be an accountant already you are unlikely to be out of work. Businesses and individuals are always going to have to complete their annual tax returns and financial accounts, and they are often not going to want to do it themselves. If you get really clever, you can just work really hard for the six months running up to the end of the financial year in April and take the summer off.

Entertainer

Street-theatre performer, children's party entertainer, stand- up comedian, musician, magician, singer – if you have a natural talent for entertaining, then working for yourself is the ideal way of going about it. Even better, you can give it a go while you are still in full-time paid employment and only make the switch when you can see the potential for making a living this way.

Project manager

Once upon a time, managing a project meant having to be in an office every day in order to keep tabs on what everyone involved was doing. Not anymore. Thanks to technology, you can now manage a project from anywhere, using interactive software tools, shared documents and communal online email and chat facilities.

Domestic services provider

There will always be a demand for services that customers can't or don't want to do themselves – dog walking, gardening, ironing shirts, as well as repairing computers, making curtains and cleaning ovens. If you can identify a market of people who are short on time, but have a desire for a certain standard of living and enjoy a high level of disposable income – a prosperous city with lots of people in well-paid jobs, for example – you could be on to a winner.

Photographer

There are all kinds of ways to turn a talent for taking good photos into a self-employed career, from taking pictures at weddings, parties and other special occasions, to portraits of families or images for business brochures, leaflets and marketing campaigns.

Leadership coach or careers counsellor

If you are interested in listening to people's stories and like the idea of helping them to achieve their true potential, you could become a leadership coach, life coach or careers counsellor. With the right qualifications you could guide people through the challenges they face at work or in their personal lives; for example, helping senior executives to get better at communicating with their team. You might choose to do this by working with a client on a one-to-one basis or by going into businesses to run workshops.

Software developer

If you enjoy working with computers and writing code then you could use your skills to help businesses maintain and upgrade their IT systems. Also sometimes known as a software engineer or systems programmer, this skill is in much demand from businesses of all sizes as computer systems grow ever more complicated. So if you know your Java from your C# then providing you keep your skills up to date there is unlikely to be a shortage of work in this area.

Handyman/woman

If you are good at working with your hands and enjoy repairing and fixing things, then you could provide a range of services to your local community. This might entail anything from mending a fence to hanging a picture or replacing a lock. You can add more skills as you progress, and if you build up a reputation for turning up on time, doing a good job and leaving the place tidy afterwards, you will be in much demand.

Driver

If you like driving and have your own car, bike or van, you could either provide a delivery service or become a taxi driver, offering a private chauffeur service or working with an established local firm. You may need to work evenings and weekends and must always ensure that your vehicle is in top condition. Demand for drivers can be unpredictable, however, so the best way to ensure a steady income is to set up a regular arrangement with individuals or local businesses that require your services.

Independent sales rep

If you are good at selling and enjoy it, you could make a living selling products or services on behalf of businesses, earning a commission every time you make a sale. Depending on what you are selling, you may be pitching to potential customers over the phone or in person at their business, and as you are working independently you can build up a portfolio of several complementary or non-competing products or services that you can sell to clients at the same time.

Illustrator

If you are great at drawing, you may be able to find a demand for your services. The best way to get noticed and find work is to create a niche – say, sketching buildings for architects, recreating courtroom scenes for newspapers or illustrating town-planning schemes for local councils. Hone your expertise and create a pool of regular clients.

Sports coach or fitness trainer

As people increasingly recognise the value of regular exercise to combat obesity and to improve general wellbeing, there is a growing need for experts to show us how to do it properly. If you enjoy playing sport or keeping fit then you could help others do the same by getting the relevant teaching qualifications and then organising individual or group lessons, either directly with customers or through a sports or fitness club, or both.

Florist

If you are creative and enjoy working with your hands, you could become a florist, designing beautiful flower arrangements for hotels and restaurants, or for important occasions such as weddings and funerals. Florists need to have a good eye for colour and co-ordination and must be able to combine practical skills with artistic talent. You may also need to be willing to travel and work odd hours, getting up early to source flowers from the market in time for a big event.

These are just a starting point. And you don't have to limit yourself to any one of them. There are hundreds of jobs which can be done by people who work for themselves. The only limit is your imagination.

TOP TIP

Study local trade directories to see the kind of services that are already being offered in your area – and, crucially, where there are gaps. If there are already thirteen portrait photographers operating in your town, you really don't want to be the fourteenth – but perhaps you could be the first pet photographer?

Chapter 5

When do you make the move?

'It is never too late to be what you might have been'

George Eliot, novelist

The next step in launching your solo career is figuring out when to take the plunge. Should you start straight out of school or when you leave university? Or is it better to wait until you are doing well in a salaried job? Or should you leave it until you are completely fed up with your job, or you have been made redundant? The good news is that any of these options are possible, as are other options too, according to which stage you are at in your career. However, there are particular advantages and challenges to taking the plunge at different points in your life, so it is important to consider the whole package before making your move. Let's take a look.

Straight out of school or university

A growing number of people are choosing to ditch the traditional employee route entirely and deciding to go it alone at the start of their working life. According to figures from the Office for National Statistics, the number of self-employed people in the UK aged between 16 and 24 increased from 104,000 in 2001 to 181,000 in 2016.

Chris Bryce, chief executive of IPSE, says: 'Many young people are leaving university with no real intention of working as an employee unless they can get the dream job at Google or Apple. Increasingly, they are coming out with a skill set that they know is marketable and has some value, and technology enables them to work from literally anywhere, so they no longer have to traipse into a dull office and work from nine till five. They also see that there is potential for earning more money than they would as a relatively junior member of staff in their first job.'

But while it might be tempting to think that you can create a successful freelance career from day one, you do have to think carefully about what you will miss out on by going it alone at this stage, and how you might be able to make up for it in other ways.

If you decide to work for yourself straight from school or university without getting a salaried job first, the two most important things you will lack are industry contacts and experience. You will need to make a real effort to start building up both – by attending events and contacting people you think might be able to help you, and by creating a strong portfolio of work (that you may have had to do unpaid) to show potential clients what you are capable of.

It will really help if you have an impressive creative talent that people are going to want to pay for, regardless of how little experience you have. It will also help if you can start developing the basis of your freelance career while you are still at school or university, so that you have something to build on when you leave.

Advantages As you are unlikely to have dependants to provide for and you don't have a job to give up, you really have nothing to lose, particularly if you are happy to live on very little in the first few years. As you are young, you are likely to be full of energy and enthusiasm and have the capacity to work hard, all of which will be immensely useful. You also have no real concept of what a regular nine-to-five job looks like, so you can create a routine and way of working which suits you. And you have time to learn new skills that clients want.

Challenges Your lack of experience may make it harder for you to find work, and without a network of industry contacts it might be more difficult to establish credibility. By opting to work for yourself now rather than later, you also miss out on the career progression that could catapult you into self-employment at a higher level later on.

Action plan Without contacts or experience to get you started, success for you will be all about creating some high-impact marketing to get you noticed. Depending on what kind of work you are offering, that might mean creating some colourful flyers or leaflets to post through people's doors, putting up some high-impact posters in your local newsagent's window, creating an eye-popping website or posting regularly on social media. Or all of the above.

While you are in a salaried job

In the past few years there has been a surge in the number of people in their forties and fifties choosing to start working for themselves. Indeed, according to the Office for National Statistics, self-employment is most commonly found among people aged between 45 and 54.

Although it can be daunting to give up a salaried job for the uncertainty of working for yourself, you also have the advantage of knowing your industry very well and having an up-to-date insight into how it operates and who the key players are.

You may also know where the freelance and self-employed opportunities might lie. Indeed, you may even be able to have some informal discussions before you leave your job with people who are in a position to commission freelance work from you, and so line up some initial work for when you start working for yourself.

Advantages By lining up work in advance you will be able to get going immediately when you start working for yourself. You will have an in-depth understanding of the market and know the right people to contact to keep the work coming in.

Challenges It can be hard to give up the security of a well-paid salaried job for the uncertainty of working for yourself, particularly as it may take a while until the income you are able to generate yourself matches the salary you have just given up. And it is not just the regular monthly pay cheque you are giving up; there may well be other perks you have to say goodbye to as well, such as pension contributions, company car and private healthcare.

Action plan While you still have your job, establish as many contacts as you can with people who might be able to give you work later, to make the transition as smooth as possible. Also save as much of your salary as possible while you are still being paid, to give you a buffer for the first few months of working for yourself.

While you are looking after young children or elderly parents

Working for yourself is an ideal option for people who are unable to commit to full-time employment in a fixed location away from home. You can fit the work around your other obligations and you can work as much or as little as you need to, when it suits you best.

Advantages If you are not currently earning much money, or indeed any, there is less pressure to instantly try to find enough work to replace a full-time salary. This means you can start small and gradually build up your freelance work channels and income stream.

Challenges If you have already spent several years out of the workplace you may lack up-to-date knowledge about the opportunities that exist for self-employed workers, so you will need to spend some time thoroughly researching your potential market.

Action plan Get in touch with everyone you have previously worked with, no matter how long ago it was, and ask them if they would be happy to meet you for a coffee and offer you some work advice. Most people will be happy to share their knowledge. You may be able to find many of the people you have lost touch with on LinkedIn (www.linkedin.com).

When you are having a mid-life (or any-time-of-life) existential crisis

It is perhaps not surprising that so many people choose to take the plunge when middle age hits. If you have spent the last twenty years working for an organisation, you may not want to spend the next fifteen to twenty years doing the same thing. And all those skills and contacts you have gained along the way are extremely marketable.

After spending so long being nice to bosses, pretending to care about the latest interim report, enduring endless tedious meetings, biting your tongue and moulding yourself to fit in with the corporate image, it can be a huge relief to throw the whole thing up in the air and take back control of what you do and how you do it.

Out with the swanky job title, company car and sharp suits, but in with a great sense of freedom at throwing off the shackles of a corporate career. Making the switch from salaried employment to working for yourself is not just like applying for a new job, it is like embarking on a whole new exciting adventure.

Advantages You can be the person you always wanted to be and live life on your terms, while you still have the energy to throw yourself into it.

Challenges After so many years of cruising through life on a salary and with defined expectations about how to act and what is required of you, going it alone might come as a bit of a shock.

Action plan Now is the time to do some exploring to find out what you really want from life. Before you quit your job, take two weeks off to go backpacking around Asia, cycling around France, walking in the Scottish Highlands or whatever takes your fancy. Talk to everyone you meet along the way to gain some new perspectives, and then start coming up with some ideas of your own.

When you are made redundant

In some ways it can be easier to make the switch to working for yourself if you are made redundant because the decision to give up your job has already been made for you. Choosing to work for yourself at this point also saves you having to go through the whole dismal process of dusting off your CV and applying for new jobs. However, being made redundant can be a brutal experience, particularly if you had no idea that it was about to happen, so it is important to stay positive, look forward and turn any hurt and anger you feel into a fierce determination to make working for yourself a roaring success. Remember, this might just be the start of something far more exciting.

Advantages You don't have to make the difficult decision to give up a salaried job and you may have received a redundancy payment which will help to keep you afloat financially until you start making money working for yourself.

Challenges Being made redundant can be a crushing experience and may have knocked your confidence, so you need to find ways to create new support networks and believe in yourself and your abilities again.

Action plan Find an upbeat positive phrase you can use to explain your situation when you get in touch with prospective clients. You don't have to use the R word; something like 'I had been looking to make a move for some time and the opportunity has now arisen to strike out on my own' will be fine.

When you retire

Retirement is the perfect opportunity to start working for yourself, particularly if you can't see yourself doing anything but playing golf and pottering around the garden for the next twenty years. It has the added bonus of providing you with additional income and keeping you mentally alert, something which experts agree can significantly improve quality of life. Best of all, if you are applying for work online through one of the freelance websites, no one need ever know how old you are, and so cannot discriminate against you. According to the Office for National Statistics, the over-65 age group experienced the biggest increase in self-employment of any age group between 2001 and 2016, increasing from 159,000 to 469,000.

The expertise you have built up over the course of your working life can be extremely valuable to companies. Xenios Thrasyvoulou, the founder and CEO of freelance website PeoplePerHour.com says: 'There are a lot of retired people on our site. They join because they have had a brilliant career and are bored doing nothing. In fact, the guy who came up with our strapline 'Job Done' was retired – he used to own three award-winning advertising agencies. It would normally be very difficult for a small business to hire someone with that level of experience, but because he was freelancing, we were able to access his expertise.'

Advantages Working for yourself means you can continue to use your skills and experience to earn an income for as long as you want to. You can do as much or as little as you choose, and by working on small projects you may be enabling small businesses to tap into your skills in a way that they would never otherwise have been able to afford.

Challenges You may be competing for work with young people who may be more tech and social-media savvy than you are, so you will have to make a real effort to keep your skills relevant and up to date.

Action plan Create a list of useful contacts from your previous job, and put the word out that you are going freelance. Consider too whether you need to adapt your personal style to a different kind of working environment.

Ultimately, the best time to take the plunge and work for yourself is when *you* decide that you want to. Working for yourself can only ever be a success if you really want to do it – because otherwise, you simply won't bother making that call or sending that email.

TOP TIP

Assess your current work situation carefully to see how you might make the most of any resources it can provide before you start working for yourself. Are there any training courses you can take or qualifications you can get before you leave? Is there a possibility you might be offered voluntary redundancy in the next few months? Could you start working for yourself as a side gig alongside your salaried job for a while until you get more established?

Chapter 6

Create the right structure

'Quality means doing it right when no one is looking'

Henry Ford, car manufacturer and industrialist

When you are starting out working for yourself there is one simple rule to stick to: the more organised you are, the better it will work out and the happier you will be.

If you are still in a job right now, whether you are planning to leave or you have been made redundant and are working out your notice, you can use the last few months of being at work to plan ahead and get everything set up so you are ready to go from day one.

Put the right business and tax structure in place

When you start working for yourself you have two main tax structures to choose from. You can either become a sole trader, meaning that you are classed as being self-employed, or you can create a limited company, meaning that you are classed as a business.

There used to be considerable tax advantages to creating a limited company rather than becoming a sole trader, but these have gradually been eroded, so it now largely depends on which structure is most suitable for the type of work you are doing and the industry you are doing it in. Some larger businesses, for example, prefer to work only with limited companies rather than sole traders.

If you become a sole trader, you will need to register for Self Assessment with HMRC, the government tax department. You will need to complete a self-assessment tax return each year detailing how much you have earned in the past year, and then pay income tax on this. The main advantage of becoming a sole trader is that there is very little paperwork involved – you simply sign up for Self Assessment and off you go.

If you create a limited company, you will become an employee of your business. You will need to complete a tax return each year and also file annual accounts. You will have to pay corporation tax on the income your business earns, and if you withdraw dividends from your business you will have to pay tax on those too. Setting up a limited company involves a fair amount of form-filling and you may need to employ an accountant to do it for you. The main advantage, however, is that your limited company is a separate legal entity, meaning that the business is liable for any debts or legal claims made against it, rather than you personally. Also, depending on the industry you are working in, operating as a business rather than as a sole trader could make you look and feel more professional, although you will need to decide whether or not that is worth the cost and administration involved.

Decide what to call yourself

Depending on the type of work you are doing and the clients you will be working for, you may choose to either create a separate brand for your work or use your own name. There is no right or wrong answer to this; it is simply down to the kind of image you want to project and what you feel would work best in your industry.

Join the relevant industry organisation

Most industries have some kind of members' organisation which provides and upholds professional standards by offering training, qualifications, certification, Continuing Professional Development (CPD) programmes and membership criteria. People working in the entertainment industry, for example, have Equity (www.equity.org.uk), chartered surveyors have RICS (www.rics.org) and psychologists have the British Psychological Society (www.bps.org.uk). In some areas membership is voluntary; for others, it is compulsory – gas engineers, for example, must be registered with the Gas Safe Register (www.gassaferegister.co.uk).

These organisations can be a great source of information and advice, and joining them can often be a good way of showing clients that you are offering a professional service, particularly if you are able to gain some form of accreditation from them. For some industries it may also be a formal requirement that you undertake their Continuing Professional Development programmes in order to be allowed to operate on a professional basis. Even if you do not need a particular qualification or endorsement, you may still find that it's worth having because it will reassure clients that you know what you are doing. I am far more likely to hire an accountant who is chartered or certified to do my tax return than someone who simply owns a calculator and says they know how to do accounts.

Get any permits you need

If you are preparing food at home or working with any kind of hazardous substances, you may need to get a permit from your local council or arrange for them to inspect your premises. Check out your local council's website for information.

Get insurance

This is not an optional extra, this is a must-have. Don't skimp on it. For the sake of a few hundred pounds a year, you can buy yourself peace of mind. There are several different kinds of insurance available, depending on the kind of service you are offering. These are the six types of insurance likely to be most relevant to you:

Professional indemnity insurance

If you offer a service or advice, for example as a consultant or accountant, this will protect you if this is incorrect and results in loss or injury to them. You may also need it if you handle data belonging to a client or work with their intellectual property. It will cover you for claims of negligence and giving poor advice, including libel and slander, malicious falsehood, misrepresentation, errors, omissions and unintentional breach of confidence. Clients may want to check that you have an up-to-date professional-indemnity policy in place before they work with you.

Public liability insurance

If you are negligent in some way, resulting in loss or injury to a member of the public, a client or a contractor, this will cover your business for any claims made against it. It is particularly important if clients or members of the public come to your work premises, but also if you visit a client's premises to carry out your work. If you accidentally drop a brick on someone's foot while building a wall for them, for example, public liability insurance will cover you for any compensation claims made against you.

Income protection insurance

If you are unable to work due to illness or an accident, this will pay you a regular weekly income until you are well enough to return to work. Depending on the policy, you would typically receive between 50 and 70 per cent of the amount you would normally earn. However, the qualifying criteria for self-employed workers can be very strict, sometimes requiring you to be unable to do any kind of work, not just the work you would normally do, so make sure you read the policy carefully and if in doubt seek expert advice.

Cyber protection insurance

Also known as e-risks insurance, this protects you against cyber and electronic risks when using the Internet and email, and provides cover for damage caused by viruses, hackers and electronic ID theft.

Buildings and contents insurance

This is to protect your home-based office, as your existing home contents insurance policy is unlikely to be sufficient to cover your work requirements, particularly if you have expensive equipment or store stock at home.

While it is possible to buy individual policies, a better plan would be to find an insurer or broker that specialises in providing policies to self-employed people and small businesses to ensure you have everything you need. You can also buy insurance packages for specific trades such as electrician, plumber and market trader, which bundle together the elements you need for your specific circumstances. Tradesman insurance, for example, is a package which will typically include cover for professional indemnity, public liability, business premises, equipment, tools, contract works, stock and plant. Ask someone you trust if they can recommend an insurance broker they use themselves.

Create a website

Whatever kind of service you are planning to offer, it is always useful to have a website, no matter how basic. A website acts as a virtual shop window, explaining to potential clients who you are, what you do and how to get in touch. These days, there are lots of website-builder sites that enable you to create a website yourself, and you don't need any expert knowledge. You just choose a template and fill in the blanks with words and pictures. I created both my business website, www.frogletproductions.com, and my personal website, www.rachelbridge.com, using WordPress (www.wordpress. com). They are both managed and hosted by GoDaddy (www.godaddy.com), but there are dozens of providers to choose from. You can also get a personalised email address to match from Google Suite (www.gsuite.google.com) – I have the email addresses enquiries@frogletproductions.com and rachel@rachelbridge.com, for example.

When designing your website, bear in mind that its primary purpose is to get you work. So make sure that it sends out a clear, coherent message about who you are and what you can do. Write a well-defined, straightforward description of yourself that sets out the services you offer, where you are located and where you are happy to undertake jobs.

Explain how you differ from the competition – are you able to provide a faster, better or more effective service than others on the market? Do you have years of valuable experience, or can you offer a specialist skill that they don't have? Make sure you include good photos too. Potential customers like to see evidence of work you have successfully undertaken, whether it is a garden, a bookshelf or a bouquet of flowers. If your work is something you can take a 'before' and 'after' photo of, such as installing a new shower, do that as well.

If customers send you nice thank-you notes or endorsements for your work, ask if you can include them on your website as testimonials.

Put your contact details on the front page as well as on the contacts page to reduce the amount of clicking and searching that people have to do. Finally, make sure that your website actually works. No one will be impressed if they get a 404-error message when they try to access your website, so use a reputable hosting service and consider paying a bit extra for protection to keep your website secure from hackers.

Get your location right

Make sure that the kind of work you want to do fits in with where you live. If you want to be a children's party entertainer, check that you live in an area that has many young children living there – a useful guide is to count how many primary schools there are. If your work will involve a lot of travelling, ensure there are good transport links near your home. If you need to attend meeting with potential clients on a regular basis, make sure it is not going to take you all day to get there and back.

Hollywood screenwriters Robert Ben Garant and Thomas Lennon nail this point in their book *Writing Movies for Fun and Profit*. They write: 'If you're serious about screenwriting, you must be in Los Angeles, California. It is the world headquarters of the movie industry. You need to have access to the studios all the time, and they need to have access to you. You have to live in LA, so that you can go to the studios and meet face-to-face. At any time.'

They know what they are talking about. The two of them have so far written nine Hollywood movies together, including *Night at the Museum, Taxi*, and *Herbie: Fully Loaded*.

Get the right kit

Get the best equipment you can afford if it is vital to your ability to do your job, whether that is a video camera, computer or sewing machine. Depending on how often it will need upgrading, you may prefer to rent or lease it, rather than buy it, but either way, investing in the best-quality kit will be worth it. A shoddy or broken piece of equipment could cost you thousands in lost earnings, plus a loss of goodwill among your clients if it results in delays or faults. The good news is that work equipment counts as work-related expenses, so can be offset against your earnings for tax purposes.

Get a big book

Buy yourself a big hardback book in which to write down all your work commissions. I have created several columns in mine for each entry, as follows:

As soon as I am given a piece of work, I write it down, together with the date it was commissioned, how much I am getting paid for it and when it is due. When the work has been done and I send out an invoice, I add the number of the invoice next to the entry. Then when it is paid, I write down the date it was settled. So simple, but so incredibly useful.

I choose to do all this in a notebook because it is easy to access and I know I will still have it if my computer stops working, but you could also do this on an Excel spreadsheet. Either way, do it. You might wonder why you are bothering when you first start working for yourself and it's easy to keep track of the work you are doing, but get into the habit right from the start. When the work starts pouring in you will be glad of it.

TOP TIP

Find out the relevant business organisation or association for your industry – there may be more than one – and check out its website for the sort of services it provides. It may run open events or evenings that you can attend to learn more.

Chapter 7

Choose your workspace

'Yours truly has never worked out of an office, and never will'

Richard Branson, entrepreneur

N ow for the fun part – sorting out a place to work in. If the service you are offering can only be done with the client present or at the client's location – if you are cutting their hair, painting their hall or mending their IT equipment, for example – then you are obviously going to be spending most of your time there. But if you are doing work which you can do by yourself and you don't have to be in the same physical space as your client, you have lots of options about where you might want to be:

Home

When you work for yourself, your home is the most obvious place to start doing it. According to the latest Labour Force Survey by the Office for National Statistics, 28 per cent of self-employed people work mainly at home.

I work from home and absolutely love it. I love the fact that I am already here, and that I don't have to spend time or money travelling anywhere else. I love that I can write at 5a.m. or 11p.m. and I love that I can do something useful – mow the lawn or hang up the washing – when I need a change of activity to provide inspiration. I love that if I suddenly remember something I need to do workwise, then no matter what time of day or night it is, I can turn on the computer and immediately sort it out. I love that I can arrange my working environment to exactly suit my needs, so I can have it as hot or as cold as I want, quiet or with music. And I especially love the fact that it doesn't cost me any money to work here, apart from the cost of keeping the lights on and higher heating bills in winter. (Depending on the kind of work you are doing, you may be able to claim back a proportion of that as expenses on your annual tax return anyway.)

However, some people dislike working from home. They dislike that there is no physical separation between work and home, and that they feel they can never truly switch off. They find it difficult to see themselves as a dynamic, ambitious, professional grown-up when they are working at the kitchen table or crouched over a desk in the spare bedroom feeling as though they are teenagers again, doing their homework. They miss the ritual of dressing up for work and going somewhere else. They miss being surrounded by other people. And they hate the distractions of the fridge and the television and the unfinished domestic chores.

The truth is, there is no right or wrong here. It's a very personal thing – you either love it or you don't, and the best way to find out is to give it a try.

Working from home – making it work for you

1. Create a space to store all your work documents, so they are not constantly getting lost around the house.

2. Make your work area an appealing place to be. Get a comfortable chair and good lighting and try your desk out in different positions to see if you prefer to be facing a wall, door or window.

3. If you think you might be distracted by household chores, close the door on the mess and work in a different room. The same goes for the television and the fridge. Put doors and space between you and them.

4. Accept that if you are the only one working from home in your street, you will end up being interrupted frequently when couriers ask you to take in your neighbours' deliveries when they are out – plus your hall will be full of other people's parcels. If you really don't want to be disturbed, unplug the doorbell or put a polite notice on the door.

5. If you have a flatmate, partner or children sharing your home, establish some house rules. Agree which room you can use to work in and make sure that this is not going to cause resentment. If your children have been used to having a playroom of their own, they might not appreciate you turning it into an office.

Advantages Cheap and convenient

Challenges Can be difficult to separate work from home and you may feel isolated and unprofessional

Tip Be careful not to convert any part of your house into a permanent workspace that can no longer be used for living purposes, because if it is regarded as formal business premises, you may be liable to pay business rates and ultimately capital gains tax if you sell your home at a profit. Your workspace should always continue to have a potential dual use.

Café

In theory, the idea of working in a café sounds wonderful. It's warm, it's pleasant, it's full of life and it's free, apart from having to buy the occasional drink. In reality, however, it can be quite stressful, because if it is busy you will be taking up valuable table space and the staff and other customers will glare at you.

Then there is the noise when parents come in with their babies and toddlers mid-morning, background music, and the problem of finding an electricity socket that you can use. And that's before you have even dealt with the problem of going to the toilet – if you leave your laptop on the table you risk someone going off with it; if you take it with you, you risk losing your place.

Ziferblat have come up with an ingenious solution in the form of cafés that charge by the minute instead of for the drink, eliminating the problem of having to buy endless coffees and being glared at. You simply pay 8p a minute for the time you spend there and the coffee and cakes are free, which means you can spend all day there if you want to. However, the downside is that they currently only have a handful of outlets, so the chances of finding one near you are limited.

Advantages Convenient and fairly cheap – although not if you end up having to buy lots of coffees and can't resist the cake

Challenges Noisy and stressful

Tip If you are planning to work this way, buy a computer with a long battery life. Cafés don't always appreciate people using their electricity sockets to recharge their equipment.

Shared office space

A shared office space has considerable advantages. You have your own dedicated desk – and phone line, if you need one – and are surrounded by other people working in the same way as you do. That gives you the friendliness and conviviality of being in an office with the freedom of working for yourself, and at a fraction of the cost of renting your own private office. As you are renting a specific desk, you can leave your stuff there overnight, and because you are with the same group of people every day you can get to know them well and they may even provide work and networking opportunities. At the very least, you will have someone to go out with for a post-work beer.

Advantages Sociable, potential work opportunities

Challenges It may be hard to find one located near to you; you may find it difficult to concentrate if everyone around you is constantly on the phone

Tip Shared office space tends to be organised on an ad-hoc local basis, so check websites and social media for information about what might be available.

Alex Mallinson works for himself creating animated content for television shows, adverts, large businesses and websites. He decided to go freelance in 2004 at the age of 26 after working for a business which made video games.

He has made several changes to his working location since he began working for himself. For the first few years he worked at home, in a house he shared with flatmates, and when he moved in with his girlfriend, he continued to do this. But his girlfriend had a full-time job in an office elsewhere and Alex discovered that it was a very different experience being on his own every day without other people around. 'I worked from home for five years on my own, and that was a terrible mistake,' he says. 'It was disastrous for my sanity and for my social muscles – they atrophied, and it was like regressing into teenage years. I would rabbit on at my girlfriend when she got home from work because I hadn't spoken to anyone all day.'

Realising he needed to make a change, Alex now rents desk space in a shared creative office above a bank in Cambridge for £150 a month. He travels there each day by bicycle and train, which takes him about thirty minutes. 'I share an office with filmmakers, Internet copywriters and content creators, and it has been transformative. The biggest thing for me is just being among people. At first, I thought I would work there maybe three or four days a week, but I now work there every day.'

He adds: 'The totally crucial thing that has improved every aspect of my life has been dividing work from home life. I just couldn't make that separation. I had a study at home and I thought that was enough. I could finish work for the day and close the door, but I would think of things and dash upstairs back to the study. Making sure that home is just for home has been one of the biggest lessons for me.'

Co-working space

The last few years have seen a big growth in the amount of co-working space available, particularly in larger towns. The main difference between a shared office and co-working space is that with the latter you do not have a dedicated desk to call your own – you simply work at one that is available. There may be lockers to store your stuff, but otherwise you take everything you need with you each time you go there.

Another difference is that if you don't want to commit to working there full-time, you can choose to do so for just a few hours a week, perhaps between meetings. There may be less requirement to sign up for a long period of time too, and greater flexibility to change how often you work there.

There are now dozens of co-working spaces in London and other major cities, with established brands including Wework (www.wework.com) and Regus (www.regus.co.uk). However, you will have to look harder the further away you are from the big cities.

When you go to check out a co-working space, count how many available electricity sockets there are and look at the opening hours – are you able to go in and work there in the evenings or at weekends if you want to?

Advantages Sociable, flexible, networking opportunities

Challenges Not having a desk of your own; may not be available where you live

Tip Before you sign on the dotted line, visit the co-working space at different times of day and on different days of the week to see how crowded or quiet it gets. Too crowded, and it may be hard to find a desk; too quiet, and it may feel strange.

Your own office

If you have to hold regular meetings for your work and prefer to conduct them in private on your own premises, you may consider renting your own office. You can furnish it in the style you wish and clients will be able to visit whenever you choose. This is an expensive option, however, and can be just as isolating as working from home, so it is worth trying out other options first before committing to this.

Advantages Privacy; gives a professional image to clients

Challenges High cost; isolation; long-term commitment required

Tip If you need a private place to meet clients on a regular basis, a growing number of venues in major towns enable you to book meeting rooms or conference rooms by the hour. Alternatively, if you simply need an office address without actually having to work there, you can hire a virtual business address which you can use on business correspondence, and they will send your post on to you.

Other spaces

Depending on where you live, you may be able to work in your local library, although this is not ideal if you need to make and take phone calls. Leisure centres and hotel lobbies are other options which often offer fairly quiet communal spaces, although both of these are unlikely to have desks or desk-height tables, so you may have to work with your laptop on your knee.

Advantages Free or very low cost

Challenges Unlikely to be able to work there all day; lack of facilities may restrict your ability to work

Tip If you need to conduct several meetings in a day, spend the day in a smart hotel lobby or café and arrange for everyone to come and meet you there, giving them back-to-back hourly time slots. You will achieve an enormous amount.

Work on the move

If your work mainly involves being on the phone with only occasional forays to your computer, it may be possible to work on the move, tapping into Wi-Fi and electricity sockets as needed.

This is the fantasy option that many people dream of, spurred on by dreamy Instagram shots of so-called digital nomads sitting on some far-flung tropical beach with their laptops on their knees, sipping cocktails, as palm trees sway against the blue skies behind them.

In reality, of course, it never quite turns out like that, partly because sand and laptops don't mix, but mostly because you are putting yourself at the mercy of technology that may or may not decide to co-operate. I have lost count of the times I have walked around a hotel car park waving my mobile phone in the air, trying in vain to find a signal, or raced around a train station trying to find a Wi-Fi connection before my train leaves. I am also completely over the experience of having to use my phone as a laptop because my computer has run out of battery and shut itself down. Trying to write a report or even a detailed email on a small phone is no fun at all. Just because it is possible, doesn't make it desirable.

Working on the move also means that you have to carry everything with you all the time, something those tantalising Instagram shots never convey. Once you are laden down with laptop, cables, mouse, tablet, charger, phone, notebook, pens, folders and glasses, you are more likely to resemble a backpacker on their gap year than a jet-setting professional. The truth is that if you are going to do this properly, you need a base to call your own, even if it is a co-working hut in Bali.

Advantages You can potentially work and earn a living while you travel the world

Challenges Total reliance on technology working properly, when and where you need it to; having to constantly carry everything you need with you

Tip Label everything with your name, email address and phone number. That way, if you leave something behind on a train, some nice fellow digital nomad will easily be able to contact you to let you know.

Of course the best thing about working for yourself is that you don't have to guess which kind of workspace is going to be your favourite – you can try out several options to see which works best for you. And then you can switch again if you change your mind.

Trevor Merriden left his job as director of a PR firm in 2012 to start working for himself. He helps firms to create content and engage with their customers, and has several clients at any one time.

Trevor started out working in a converted shed in the garden of his home in St Albans, but then switched to renting an office of his own at a cost of £600 a month. He has now swapped again to a desk in a shared office space at a cost of £200 a month, and he plans to alternate this with working in his shed.

'I spent the first four years sitting in my shed in the back garden because I wanted to keep the overheads as low as possible,' Trevor explains. 'But then I got to a point where I wanted to go into a proper grown-up office. I felt like I needed a bit of separation from the house. But now I have decided that wasn't really necessary, so I have found a shared office.'

Trevor has also realised he likes the freedom of being able to change location every now and then: 'If I feel as though I have worked too many days in the office, I will make sure I go and work somewhere else. I just like a bit of variety. Sometimes I want to work by myself and sometimes I don't. If I need to do deep-thinking work, I can be by myself, but if I want to do emails and feel more sociable, I will go to the shared office.'

TOP TIP

Wherever you choose to work, you will need to keep your data secure with malware and security software to minimise the risks of using public Wi-Fi. Bear in mind that you will also need to back up everything. If you lose your laptop, you really don't want to lose your work too.

———————

Chapter 8

How to find work

'Whenever you are asked if you can do a job, tell 'em,
"Certainly I can!" Then get busy and find out how
to do it'

Theodore Roosevelt, American president

When you work for yourself you can't just hope that projects, bookings or commissions will magically appear. You have to go out and find them, especially in the early days when you are getting started.

There are many ways of sourcing work. Depending on the kind of work you are looking for, you can try one or more of the approaches below.

1. Pitch to your existing network

In other words, contact everyone you have ever known – friends, friends of friends, friends' parents, neighbours, former colleagues, previous bosses, industry contacts, former teachers, people who used to work in the next department to you, people you used to chat to in the lift, people you met once at a party, people you exchanged business cards with at a conference ...

Don't hold back – getting work from someone you already have a connection with, no matter how loose or tenuous, is the single most effective way to get your freelance career off the ground. That's because the link bestows trust and confidence and people always feel far more comfortable about hiring someone they have a connection with and who they feel they can trust. So spread yourself as far and as wide as you can.

The simplest way to get in touch is to send a personal email. Remind them who you are, explain that you have started working for yourself, and tell them what you do and how you can help them. Keep it short and to the point and write it in such a way that the recipient can forward your message to other people they know who might be interested in hiring you. Create and attach a one-page profile of yourself which sets out clearly what you have been up to for the past few years and any experience and qualifications you have. Some businesses do not allow attachments to be opened, so also paste the profile into the body of the email, mentioning in your message that it is there.

Tip If you don't have someone's email address, connect to them on LinkedIn; if they accept your request, their personal email address will appear under their contact information.

Be prepared to drink lots of coffee

Accept that when you are just starting out working for yourself, you may need to spend a lot of time having coffees and meetings that don't directly lead to any actual work. This can be frustrating, especially as you are now spending your own money on travel and drinks, but these meetings are a necessary first step towards your goal. The more people who know you are available for freelance work, the better, and as you explain to them what you are looking to do, it will also help you to clarify this in your own mind. Regard the process as a paper chain of people who can pave the way to the next introduction, until, hopefully, you reach the ultimate prize: the person who can offer you real paid work.

Don't ignore the obvious

It may be that your former employer is able to offer you free-lance work, perhaps doing some of the tasks you previously did in a salaried job for them. This is particularly likely if the business was forced to make redundancies because they no longer have enough work to employ someone full-time, but the work still needs to be done. If you were a researcher for an organisation, for example, perhaps you could become a freelance researcher, while also taking on work from other clients.

There is one point to note, however: HMRC, the government tax department, is very suspicious of people who leave their salaried jobs and are immediately hired back by the same company to do exactly the same job, and there have been several high-profile court cases resulting in big fines. This is because this kind of arrangement can look as though you or your employer are trying to avoid paying the right amount of tax and National Insurance contributions, even if that is not the case. So if you are taking on work from your previous employer, make sure that you do it in the correct way and are not simply doing the job of an employee. See page 131 for further details, and if in doubt, seek independent legal advice.

2. Create an online presence

Everyone spends an enormous amount of time online these days, so you may be able to find work by creating an Internet presence for yourself.

Join an online trade or craft directory

If you are providing a specific trade, you can pay a monthly fee to register with an online trade directory such as Trustatrader. com or Checkatrade.com. You will then be able to create a profile on their site describing the service you offer and your contact details, so that if a potential customer searches the site looking for a tradesperson like you in their local area, you will come up as one of the options.

As well as providing you with work, directories like these can help you build up a reputation in the market because customers who hire you through the sites are asked to leave feedback and a review of your work, giving you a cumulative score for other potential customers to see.

To be eligible to join, you will need to have a certain level of experience in your trade and will have to undergo a background assessment which will check your identity, qualifications, insurance and references from previous customers.

If you are offering a traditional craft such as basket weaving and woodcarving, you can join the Heritage Crafts Association (www.heritagecrafts.org.uk) for a small annual fee and create a profile on their Makers Directory, an online directory of members who are practising craftspeople. Your profile can include details of your work and contact information.

Before you join one these sites, put yourself in your customers' shoes and search for your trade or craft in your area.

What kind of competition is there? Can you match the range of services others are offering? Is there something that you can provide that might give you the edge and persuade someone to use you rather than them?

Once you sign up, monitor your membership regularly to check that it is providing you with more work than it is costing you in monthly fees, and giving you the kind of customers and reputation that you want.

Get active on social media

Love it or loathe it, social media is a great way of finding potential customers. You can use it to tell people about the services you provide, offer promotions and discounts, announce events you are holding and give them an easy way to get in touch with you, whether to ask questions or advice or comment on what you do.

You can also use social media as a way of providing potential customers with real examples of what you do – photos you have taken, clothes you have made, events you have organised, for example.

Decide which social-media channels are going to be most relevant for the customers you are trying to attract and create an account for each of them. Are they most likely to be on LinkedIn, Twitter or Facebook? Now start working it. Follow potential clients or clients, like and share their posts, post content of your own that you think they might find interesting, share relevant content that other people have written about your industry, message them directly to see if they would like to discuss what you can do for them.

Once you have created your accounts, make sure you keep them active and up to date. You will not give a good impression to prospective customers if they look neglected.

3. Advertise your services IRL (in real life)

Traditional forms of advertising such as flyers, leaflets and posters may feel outdated compared to the modern whizz-bang power of Google search, but for certain types of work they can still be an extremely effective, low-cost way of getting clients or customers.

That's because while a Google search is ideal for someone who is actively looking for something they already know they want, leaflets, flyers and posters tell people about services they may not have even considered.

For this reason, this method works particularly well if you are providing something that makes people's lives easier and more enjoyable, such as domestic, health-and-beauty or handyman services. While it might have never occurred to someone that they might want any of these, an eye-catching leaflet pushed through their door might just inspire them to give it a go.

Research in 2018 by the Direct Marketing Association found that 60.5 per cent of people looked at, read or glanced at flyers and leaflets that came through their letter boxes, while 16 per cent put them to one side to look at later. And unlike a Google search result, a leaflet can be pinned onto a notice-board, kept in a pocket until needed or passed on to a friend.

Here's how to advertise your services in the most effective way:

Research and understand your potential market

Think hard about the kind of clients most likely to give you work, and where they are most likely to be found. If you are offering a dog-walking service, for example, you might want to create a leaflet to leave in your local veterinary surgery or pet shop; if you provide gardening services, your flyer would be better off being distributed door to door to houses with large gardens.

Get the message across

People have very short attention spans, so make sure your flyer, leaflet or notice tells them everything they need to know in an instant – price, location and how long the service takes. Use bright colours, short words and, ideally, a catchy brand name or slogan to make it memorable.

4. Take the direct approach

One way to find work is to simply draw up a list of potential clients and contact them directly to offer your services. It can be a tough sell because you are effectively 'cold-calling' them with no prior introduction, but if you have a compelling pitch and are prepared to put the effort in, then it might deliver results. Here's how to improve your chances of success:

Do your research

Take the time to identify the kind of businesses or individuals most likely to say yes. Are they going to be small firms or large corporates? Will they be based in a particular sector or run in a certain way? The better you can pin down an image of your ideal client, the less time you will waste. Keep an eye too on any online or trade magazines covering the industry you are targeting, for information that might indicate where opportunities for work are. If a new music festival has just been awarded funding, for example, your skills as an event organiser or caterer might be of interest to them.

Speak the same language

Every industry has its own words and phrases it uses to describe things, so make sure you use them correctly to show that you know what you are talking about. If you are offering your services as a website developer, for example, make it clear that you know all about PHP, MySQL, CSS, JavaScript, WordPress Codex, template design, content-management systems, plugin integration, WordPress migration and so on – assuming that you do, of course.

Give yourself labels

People are busy. They probably don't have time to do their own research on you and so will take the version that you present of yourself. A simple way of doing this is to adopt two or three labels which you can use when you introduce yourself, either by email or in person, to provide people with a shorthand way of understanding who you are and what you stand for. Your labels might be where you studied, where you worked previously, interesting things you have done. Ideally, they will be well-known brand names associated with your work to provide reassurance, security and context and to position you more effectively in the bigger picture than you alone can provide. My labels are Cambridge University (where I studied), the *Sunday Times* (where I worked) and the Edinburgh Fringe festival (I wrote and performed two solo shows there). The more they can spark a sense of familiarity, understanding and connection, the more effective they will be in opening the door to establishing a relationship with a potential client.

Show that you really understand what they do

It's important to demonstrate that you have actually bothered to find out something about a potential client or their company before you get in touch, otherwise it will feel like an indiscriminate mass 'cut-and-paste' email or approach, which isn't going to impress anyone.

If you are getting in touch with an individual who creates a regular podcast, for example, or who spoke eloquently at an event, mention it in your email – and make sure that you get the name of the podcast or event right.

Carol Lewis is the deputy editor of the property and personal finance sections of *The Times* and regularly commissions work from freelancers. She says: 'You wouldn't believe how many people don't have the first idea about the stories we run or the sort of thing that will interest us. I have even had people emailing me at *The Times* saying, Dear Carol, I regularly read the *Telegraph* …'

Be generous with your suggestions and ideas

Businesses and individuals don't always know what kind of work they need done to achieve their specific goals, so it is up to you to suggest ways in which you might help them.

If you are pitching to a business, keep in mind that regardless of the kind of enterprise it is, all businesses share a common goal, which is to sell more stuff to more customers. So if you can suggest specific ways in which they might do that – through better software systems, improved technology, marketing, promotion, customer interaction, social media – that will make it a lot easier for them to say yes.

If you are pitching to an individual, consider offering some free tips and advice that will be instantly useful to them in the area in which they are seeking help.

Thomas Mellor works for himself as a tennis coach in Cheltenham, giving individual and group lessons to adults and children. He gives group lessons at a tennis club without payment in return for being able to use its facilities and then finds paid work giving private lessons by chatting to prospective clients while they are at the club.

He is always happy to give potential clients free coaching advice to show them the difference that his knowledge and expertise could make to their game.

Thomas explains: 'I am always happy to help. You need to be able to show people that you know what you are talking about and that you care what you are talking about. I love coaching because it can make a big difference to someone's game, especially when you get people who are really focused and keen.'

Thomas finds that taking the time to chat to people in person is by far the most effective way to get new clients, with roughly seven in every ten of those he talks to typically signing up for private lessons: 'I have found that the way to be successful in this job is to be sociable and talk to people. There are always new people wanting to learn how to play tennis so it is just a matter of working out who would be interested. I have left social media alone because I find that people need to get to know you, and as good as social media can be, it is not quite the same as meeting someone in person and having a conversation with them.'

Thomas says it is important to keep talking to prospective new clients even when he has a full schedule: 'At the moment I am happy with the number of hours I am coaching, but you still have to be on the ball. One thing I learned from the very beginning is that there are a lot of tennis coaches and it is very competitive, so you have to keep new clients coming in just in case somebody leaves. It is an ongoing process.'

Follow up promptly

If potential clients respond to you in a positive way, immediately arrange to either meet them in person or have a further conversation with them to discuss their interest in more depth. Do this even if they say they don't have any immediate work for you, because often a conversation can spark off ideas for work or projects that they hadn't previously considered, and because six months later when they do have some work, they will hopefully remember you and get in touch.

5. Check out freelance job sites

The past few years have seen the emergence of several websites which offer freelance work, including PeoplePerHour (www.peopleperhour.com) and Upwork (www.upwork.com). People and businesses post projects on the sites and you can browse through and bid for them. You can also post profiles of yourself and the skills you have on the sites, so that potential clients can contact you directly with offers of work. Some projects are offered with a fixed price, while for others you must say how much you would need to be paid to do the work.

Some websites will also email you with details of recommended jobs that they think you would be well suited for as they arise.

The big advantage of these websites is that they list available work that you would never find out about otherwise. They can also be a great way of dipping your toe in the water and taking on a small project in your spare time to find out first-hand if this is a way of working that you would enjoy.

The downside is that with so many people bidding for each project, you may find yourself wasting a lot of time applying for work that you never get. The other challenge is that many of the projects don't pay very well because they don't need to. PeoplePerHour, for example, currently has more than 74,000 freelancers listed on its site, many of whom will be competing for the same work that you want to do. While clients are not obliged to take the lowest bid, they are far more likely to go for a lower offer than a higher one.

Here are some tips on how to improve your chances of getting work through these sites:

Give yourself time to register and create a profile

Creating a profile on these freelance work sites is not something you can do in five minutes, particularly as you need it to look good enough to appeal to prospective clients. You will need to decide on the skills you can offer and how much you want to charge per hour, and you may have to upload certificates which prove that you have these skills. You can also choose to create and upload a video of yourself to give people a better idea of what you are really like. Try to make your profile stand out and be memorable in some way – you are up against a lot of competition.

Research the site before choosing your hourly rate

As part of your profile you must choose an hourly rate for the skills you offer. This can be hard to do, particularly if you don't tend to measure your work by the hour, so take the time to look at what other people are charging and then decide where you would like to position yourself on the scale. The hourly rate for a software developer on PeoplePerHour, for example, ranges from £7 to £250 per hour. Bear in mind that you will also be charged a service fee by the website for any work you get, which can cost up to 20 per cent of your earnings. (For more advice on setting your prices, see Chapter 9.)

Make sure your profile is exactly as you want it to be before submitting it

It can take a week to get your application processed by the website and posted up on the site, and every time you make a change to your profile it has to be re-sent and is put to the back of the queue. So do your proofreading first – or be prepared to pay a fee to fast-track your application.

Stay on top of it

With so many freelancers listed on these sites, you cannot rely on prospective clients finding you and getting in touch to offer you work. You need to be proactive and apply for any suitable projects yourself – and then keep on applying for new projects every few days.

Be picky

If you are just starting out, you may be happy to take on projects that do not pay very well, to gain experience or simply to test out this way of working. However, if you are serious about creating a viable freelance career that can provide sufficient income to support you, you will need to be a bit selective about what you feel is actually worth bidding for because some of them pay extremely low fees. For example, I discovered a project asking someone to write a 400-word description of a product for a website in return for a fixed fee of £6. And there was another job asking for someone urgently to write 3000 words, offering a total fee of £18. No thanks.

Bear in mind too that if it is going to take you an hour to write a pitch to win a specific project, that is time you could have spent earning money elsewhere.

TOP TIP

Hire a professional photographer to take a series of photos of you in different poses, which you can use for online profiles, to apply for membership of an industry organisation or to include in a leaflet or brochure. Don't skimp by getting a friend to take a photo on their phone – this is a marketing tool and so you need it to look good.

———————

Chapter 9

How much should you charge?

*'The greatest risk to man is not that he aims too high
and misses, but that he aims too low and hits'*

Michelangelo, painter and sculptor

One of the hardest things about working for yourself is having to decide how much to charge for your services. The delight of finding a client who wants to hire you for an interesting project is quickly followed by panic when they say the dreaded words, 'So how much do you charge?'

Of course, some people never have this problem, because the areas they work in operate on predetermined rates. If you are offering a service to the general public, the price you can realistically charge will already have been largely set by your competitors. If the going rate for a pedicure is £25, you will have to be a pretty amazing pedicurist, or come up with something radically better, to be able to charge much more.

For the rest of us, however, work can show up in all sorts of shapes and sizes and time frames, which means having to price projects on a case-by-case basis. It's not much fun: quote too high and you risk pricing yourself out of the job, too low and you end up being disappointed in yourself, disliking the person you are working for and feeling cross all the way through the project because you could have earned more money. There are few things guaranteed to ruin your day more than naming your price and getting the response: 'Great, that sounds extremely reasonable – when can you start?' When my freelance friend Liz once named her daily rate, the client chuckled and said, 'Gosh, we can certainly manage that.'

But even though it is an imprecise science, there are several steps you can take to make the process easier. Here's a guide to help you navigate this difficult area.

Use a familiar fee structure

Look at how people in your industry typically charge. Is it by the hour, by the day, or by the project? Or by a different metric altogether? Unless the way you charge is going to be part of your unique selling point – you may hope to win work by offering a service that is traditionally charged by the hour for a total all-in fee, say – it makes sense to quote in a way that clients will understand and be familiar with.

If you are providing your services to markets that operate in different ways, create a selection of rates to suit their various needs, such as an hourly rate, a daily rate, a fee per session, per haircut, per joke, per tweet ... I generally offer clients a choice of rates – per word, per project, per day, per book (for ghost-writing), per event (for making speeches and running workshops or panel sessions) or a monthly retainer rate.

Sometimes it will be obvious which rate to use from the type of work being offered; other times you can negotiate this with the client. If I am asked to write a large number of articles for a website, for example, they may prefer to pay me by the word, for the entire project or with a monthly retainer. You can tweak your rates as you go along and get a better understanding of your worth, but clients do like to know actual figures upfront. They don't want to deal with someone who umms and ahhs and apologises and prevaricates and says they will get back to them; they want to use someone who acts in a calm, professional, businesslike way, giving them real numbers to consider.

If you are really desperate for clues about how much to charge, you could always bat the question back to the client – something along the lines of 'What's your budget?' But that might give the impression that either you are not very confident of your own worth or that you are new to all this and don't really know what you are doing. And they are unlikely to confess to a huge budget anyway. This strategy perhaps works best if you are dealing with an intermediary rather than directly with the client.

Check out the competition

If you are selling a service direct to the public, check out competitors' websites to find out how much they charge for their services. You can then decide if you are going to be offering a similar level of service, a more expensive premium version or a cheaper, more basic one. Remember that your location will make a big difference to how much you can charge – as a general rule, you will be able to charge more in London and other prosperous areas, although your overhead costs are likely to be higher.

Some industry bodies also provide guidance on fees. Here are some useful ones:

- **Home Advice Guide** (www.homeadviceguide.com) provides guidelines on how much plumbers, painters and electricians charge on average, with regional variations, as well as figures for specific projects, such as installing an electric shower or removing a chimney.

- **IT Jobs Watch** (www.itjobswatch.co.uk) publishes a list of the current rates being offered for IT contract work.

- **Incorporated Society of Musicians** (www.ism.org) provides recommended rates for music teachers and surveys of fees paid to musicians and accompanists.

- **Cogs Agency** (www.cogsagency.com) lists freelance day rates for a range of jobs within the digital and design industries.

- **National Union of Journalists** (www.nuj.org.uk) publishes a guide to freelance rates paid for work in areas including broadcasting, writing, editing, photography, online digital media, design, public relations, crosswords, cartoons and translations.

- **Gardeners Guild** (www.thegardenersguild.co.uk) offers advice on fees for self-employed gardeners.

- **Society for Editors and Proofreaders** (www.sfep.org.uk) suggests minimum fee rates for skills such as proofreading and copy-editing.

- **Writers' Guild** (www.writersguild.org.uk) lists minimum rates as agreed with organisations such as the BBC and ITV for scriptwriters and playwrights.

Know your ballpark

Here's a very rough guide to the kind of rates that clients or customers will pay for work, at the time this book was written. Some are taken from the sources mentioned above, although do bear in mind that the actual rates you will be able to charge depend enormously on many different factors, such as where you live, whether you are operating in a city or rural location, how much experience you have, how strong the competition is, how established the client is and whether the company you will be working for recognises industry recommendations. Rates will also change over time to reflect an increasing or decreasing demand for different kinds of services. Always do further research before using industry-recommended rates to ensure that they are a fair reflection of reality in your area:

- IT consultant: £350–600 per day

- Business consultant: £300–1000 per day

- Plumber or electrician: £40–60 per hour

- Handyman: £10–20 per hour

- Freelance journalist: 20–50p per word

- Website designer: £20–75 per hour

- Tennis coach: £20–45 per hour

- Gardener: £15–30 per hour

- Nanny: £10–16 per hour

- Social-media manager: £200–300 per day

- Mobile hairdresser: £25–45 for a cut and blow dry

- Painter and decorator: £100–170 per day

- Photographer: £200–750 per day

You could also try looking at freelance job websites such as PeoplePerHour.com to get an idea of what people charge to do similar services as you. But bear in mind that some of the rates on offer from prospective clients on these sites can be quite low.

Don't do salary division sums

Don't try to work out what to charge by taking your old salary and working backwards to calculate your hourly or daily rate. It is highly unlikely that you will consistently work the same number of hours each week for yourself as you did when you were an employee, which means that you will need to charge significantly more than simply dividing your annual salary by 52 (weeks) and then, say, 40 (hours). What's more, clients expect to pay more for a concentrated piece of work done within a short timescale, particularly if it requires specialist skills, than for an ongoing employee.

Factor in the cost of your raw materials

If you are offering a service that requires the use of raw materials that you will have to buy yourself, make sure you know how much this is going to cost you and factor it into your fee.

Lizzie Bett trained at Leiths School of Food and Wine and spent a decade cooking for clients all over the world, including the Ferrari Formula One team, before establishing herself as a caterer in Brighton, Sussex. She creates innovative food for events of all sizes from festivals and weddings to small dinner parties.

When Lizzie is asked to quote a price for catering an event she starts by working out how much the raw ingredients for the food will cost. She then adds in the other costs she will incur, such as hiring large-scale kitchen equipment and casual waiting staff to help her on the day. Next, she works out how many days of preparation the event will involve, in addition to the event itself. Finally, she adds a profit margin on top. Lizzie has a specific profit figure in mind that she would ideally like to make for a day's work, although competition from other caterers means that she doesn't always achieve this. 'I tend to work it out backwards,' she explains. 'I decide how much money I want to make from an event and then I add on how much it will cost me to buy in the ingredients and other costs. I know roughly what my suppliers charge and so I decide what I want to cook and then I can work it out from there.'

This method also means that Lizzie is able to adjust her fee to reflect personal circumstances. She will often charge more for weekend events because they take her away from being able to spend time with her family, but she may accept less for prestigious events which will raise her profile or for particularly fun events, such as catering for a wedding in France.

Like other caterers, Lizzie often finds herself having to negotiate her fee with potential clients, and if they don't want to pay what she quotes, she may suggest fewer courses or a simpler menu. However, she has learned from experience that it is sometimes better to walk away than accept a job which pays very little money: 'I have got thirty years of experience doing this and I need to be happy with what I can walk away with after an event, otherwise it is just not worth it. The difference between doing something for £100 less can make you really unhappy when you are doing it.'

In addition to working the sums out for yourself, depending on the type of industry you are in, it may also make sense to separate out the price of your raw materials and costs when preparing a quote for a client. This way it will be clear how much they are actually paying for your services to do the job and how much they would have to pay for raw materials anyway if they chose to do the job themselves. If you are painting someone's house, for example, consider quoting separately for the paint they will need and give them a choice of quality – do they want the more expensive branded paint for this amount or the generic trade version for that amount? They don't have to actually get the paint themselves; once they have made a choice, you can provide it as part of your service to them.

Pay attention to how long work takes you to do

When you are starting out, it can be really hard to know how long a project is going to take you. So if you are charging by the hour or by the day, you pretty much have to rely on guesswork to come up with a fee for the work, particularly as clients are understandably wary of open-ended budgets and like to know from the outset how much a project is going to cost them. So for the first few projects, keep a note of the time you spend doing them, so that you get better at quoting a fee for future work.

Know your minimum rate

Keep a mental note of the absolute minimum you would need to be paid to get involved in any new project. The supermodel Linda Evangelista famously said that she never got out of bed for less than $10,000, and while your rate may not quite match hers, you do have to know the point below which it simply isn't worth your while.

David Prosser used to be the business editor of the *Independent* and is now a freelance journalist and corporate writer. He is generally paid a fixed rate for his journalism work, but has to set his own rates for the corporate work he does: 'Having to decide how much to charge is one of the tough things about working for yourself,' he says. 'It is not like having an office job where you can benchmark your salary against average salaries in the organisation. I now have a set of rates – depending on what the work is, I might charge per word or per day or I might charge a fixed fee for a project. But I have developed that over time by instinct, rather than anything scientific. There is an element of trial and error.'

David is always happy to take a lower rate if he feels that a project might benefit him in some other way, but now that he has built up a steady stream of work, he has become more confident about saying no to work that doesn't pay enough: 'These days I am a bit more hard-nosed about it. I get calls from time to time from publications in other countries asking me to write something and if they don't want to pay my rate, I have got better at saying, "I'm really sorry, but it's just not worth my time." I don't like doing that because nobody likes turning away work, but I think you do have to put a value on your time, particularly if you are lucky enough to be busy.'

Don't work for free

Be very careful about doing work for free, no matter how nicely someone asks. If you are doing it for a charity or a good cause, then fantastic, go ahead. And it is fine to offer some free guidance or advice to help potential clients make up their mind about whether to go ahead and hire your services. But don't ever be persuaded to do the actual work you would normally charge a fee for, for free, simply because someone 'doesn't have a budget', or because of the vague promise that it will 'boost your profile'. It is for you to decide whether your profile needs boosting, not someone who is trying to secure your services without paying for them. And even if it does succeed in raising your profile a bit, you should still be paid for the work you are doing because you are providing a professional service that has a value. Unless there is a tangible, non-monetary benefit to you for doing the work without being paid for it, such as introducing you to someone you have always wanted to meet or taking you to a place you have always wanted to visit, just say no.

Be brave and bold

Even when you know exactly what you should be charging, it can be excruciating having to discuss it in person with someone. It takes a supremely confident person not to wilt under the pressure of that imagined sharp intake of breath. As a result, many people who work for themselves end up under-charging simply to get the conversation over with quicker.

One freelance friend, who had better remain nameless, finds the whole process of discussing payment so painful that he will go to almost any lengths to avoid it. As a result, he ends up doing a lot of work for hardly any money (in his case, this is doing cookery demonstrations) simply because when people ask him to do things he is too embarrassed to bring up the subject of how much they should pay him. In one particularly awful instance, when asked directly what he would charge for a cookery demonstration at an event, my friend was so overcome with embarrassment that he mumbled he would be happy to do it for nothing.

It is important to remember that people take price as an indicator of quality, whether they are buying a new pair of shoes, booking a hotel room or hiring a freelance worker. So if you are asking for less than you ought to be, you are basically telling the person who wants to hire you that you are not very good at what you do. Think about it; it's not the greatest message to be giving out. What's more, they may well make a mental note to call someone else more senior when a more prestigious project comes up.

Know your worth

People who are just starting out working for themselves often feel they should set low rates because they don't want to look too pushy. But that is a mistake. If you are good at what you do, then don't be afraid to charge accordingly. It is a lot easier to lower your rates if you have set them too high than it is to raise them if you have set them too low.

Luis Costa has been a freelance photographer for twelve years, mostly taking pictures of products for websites and catalogues. He also takes his own photos which he sells through his website. He became a professional photographer for a photo agency after leaving university and then worked as a creative director in London advertising agencies before becoming a freelance photographer when his children were born. Based in Hertfordshire, Luis gets work largely through word of mouth, either from advertising agencies or directly from retailers and supermarkets. He has developed a reputation for being very good at what he does and hardly ever has to redo a shot.

Luis says: 'One client called me and said they had a photographer who was cheaper than me. I have a fixed day rate and this photographer was offering to do the job for less than a third of the rate I charge. I said, "Right, OK, well, good luck with that" – because if I was going to charge as little as that I might as well stay in bed; there is so much work involved and it was just not worth it to me. The client tried the other photographer, but two weeks later they called me and asked me to carry on working with them at my usual rate, because it turned out that the other photographer had no idea how to light products properly and didn't really know what he was doing.'

Master the art of self-control

When you have told someone how much you want to be paid for a project, shut up. Do not, under any circumstances, jump in with a lower offer before they have even had a chance to respond. If they want to negotiate, they will. You don't have to do it for them. How hardball you want to play it depends entirely on how desperate you are for the work. If it is really important to you, then you may need to accept less than you had hoped for. If you are prepared to walk away if the rate you are offered doesn't match your expectations, then it can go one of two ways: if they are sufficiently keen to hire you, then you may end up getting what you wanted anyway, or you may have to walk away empty-handed.

Don't be vague

Make sure you agree all payments upfront before you start work, to avoid any disputes later, including any expenses required to complete the task, such as travel and equipment costs. If you are working on an hourly or daily fee, make sure you also agree upfront in writing – in an email or a letter – roughly how long the project will take, so there are no surprises for the client at the end.

Make sure that you are actually going to be paid

It sounds obvious, but it is always worth checking that they are not expecting you to work for free. If a client has asked you to write a proposal to win them work from a third party, for example, it could be that you are only going to get paid if the proposal you have written is successful in securing the work. It is up to you whether you choose to do this, and whether or not you feel it would be worthwhile, but do ensure that you know exactly what the deal is before you agree to write the proposal.

I'm embarrassed to admit that this actually happened to me. I was asked to write a proposal for a small company that a friend occasionally worked for and, for some reason, I never agreed a fee upfront. I thought that as it was the first time I had worked for them, and because my friend had said good things about them, I would be happy with their standard rate.

It was only when I sent them the finished piece, which had taken me several days to write, and asked how much I should put on the invoice, that they told me they wouldn't be paying me anything; they would only pay me for any subsequent work if their client decided to go ahead with the project I'd written the proposal for. Needless to say, their client didn't go ahead with the project and I never heard from them again.

TOP TIP

Create a menu of your fees and charges as a one-page A4 Word document or PDF that you can send out to people who request it. Also, practise stating your fees to a friend or family member, so that you will be able to say the numbers to a potential client with confidence and without apology.

Chapter 10

Ensuring client satisfaction

'You are what you do, not what you say you'll do'

Carl Jung, psychiatrist

O f course, getting and doing the work is only half the story. You also need to make sure that your clients or customers are happy with what you do, otherwise you are not going to be working for yourself for very long.

If your client or customer is not impressed with the service you have provided, then they won't want to hire you again, and they won't recommend you to other potential clients either. Depending on the type of industry you are in, they might express their dissatisfaction more publicly too, by posting a poor review or negative feedback online or on social media. And once that happens, it is really hard to get back on track.

Fortunately, there is much you can do to prevent this horror scenario from unfolding. Here are some guidelines.

Make sure you completely understand what you are being asked to do

When a client hires you, be careful not to make assumptions about what you are supposed to be doing. Go over everything in detail with them and double-check anything you are not sure about: how many people you are cooking for; how many designs they want to see for their kitchen; how many pages long the report should be and so on. Wherever possible get everything in writing, both for the sake of clarity and in case there is any dispute further down the line. Make sure too that you are absolutely clear about when you need to deliver the work, and if relevant, how you will deliver it. If you are still in doubt about anything, go back and check again. Clients would always rather have a second conversation to clarify any confusion than to have to deal with problems later.

Don't promise more than you can deliver

When you start to work for yourself, it is tempting to say yes to everything that comes your way because you have no idea when more work might come along. But agreeing to take on work you already know you won't be able to do very well is a terrible idea. You will not only upset the client and wreck what could have been a long, beautiful relationship, you will also end up demoralised and lose confidence, just at a time when you need to be operating at your shiny best. Be honest about what you can and can't do – if the client really likes you and wants you on board, it may be that you get the work anyway, just tailored to what you can take on.

Get the tone right

If you are not sure of the right style or tone to adopt, ask the client for examples of the work you are doing for them – a copy of a menu from a previous event, last year's version of the report you are writing. Do some research yourself too. If your client is a business, check out their website to see the image they present of themselves and go online to see if they have ever been written about in a newspaper or online. The more you can reflect the client back to themselves, the more your work will fit in with their image and culture, and the more comfortable they will feel about hiring you.

Communicate

It sounds simple and obvious, but it is the biggest thing that can make the difference between a happy client and a disgruntled one. When they are paying you to do some work, and especially if you are not based in the same physical location as them, they want to be able to talk to you, as and when they want. Clients get nervous if they don't know what is going on. So respond quickly to their emails and phone calls, and make sure you communicate with them throughout the project, particularly if you are working on an extended commission lasting several weeks, or if your work depends on finding external resources, such as locating the right props for a photo. Address their queries straight away and if something is not working out – perhaps you haven't been able to speak to someone that you had hoped to – let the client know immediately, so that they can make other suggestions or rework the project in some way.

Xenios Thrasyvoulou, founder and CEO of freelance jobs website PeoplePerHour.com, says: 'We have found consistently that it is really important for freelancers to have good communication skills. In fact, 90 per cent of the time when there is a falling out between the freelancer and the company hiring them, it is down to communication. It is rarely to do with the actual delivery of the work. If freelancers communicate at the beginning of a project, throughout the project and at the end of it, then things go better. This is true for any kind of freelancing, whether it is tech work, design work or translations.'

Accept that the first project for a new client may require extra effort

The first job for a client is always the toughest because you are entering uncharted territory and both sides need to learn how to work together. Be prepared to put in extra effort to ensure that it is a success – because if you don't get the first booking or commission right, there aren't going to be any more. The good news is that this effort will more than pay off. Once you have done one piece of work that a client likes, they are likely to ask you to do another.

Be helpful

Sometimes you may have to redo work – not because you didn't get it right the first time, but because someone higher up the organisation has changed their mind about how they want the project to look. And unless the changes are substantial, you are unlikely to get paid extra money for doing them. Don't get grumpy or cross; just accept that this is the nature of freelance work and make the changes promptly and willingly.

Meet the deadline

It doesn't matter how fantastic and amazing your work is – if you deliver it late to the client, they will not be happy. A deadline is a deadline and if you cannot do the work when it is supposed to be done, you will not be asked to do more. Clients want to hire people who will make their lives easier, not harder, so be prompt, be accurate and, above all, be reliable. Show up on time to coach them or fix their tap or paint their fence; send the website content when you said you would. The more they feel they can trust you not to let them down, the more promising the relationship will be.

If you know you won't have time to do the work that a client is offering you, say so and explain why. It is far better to turn work down than to fail to deliver it on time.

Sarah Kane, who does translation work for art-history publications, says: 'If I am offered work that I don't think I will manage to deliver by the deadline my clients want, I will tell them I am really sorry – I am interested in their project, but because of other work commitments I am not going to be able to do it. When I started out, I thought I had to accept everything going because otherwise people wouldn't come back to me, but I realise now that they respect me more for being honest. Sometimes they will be able to offer me an extended deadline so that I can still do the work anyway, but even if they can't, they always come back with other work.'

Go the extra mile

Don't just do the bare minimum for a project. Always ask yourself if there is anything extra you could be doing to make your clients feel more relaxed about the process.

Abby Gregory, the dog walker from Cheltenham, takes photos and videos of the dogs she looks after and puts them up on social media, so that their owners can see what their pets are doing when they are away from them. She says: 'I have a Facebook page, and every day I put up photos of what the dogs have been up to that day. My clients seem to really appreciate it. They really like the fact that they can see where their dog has been and who they were with. It is so much nicer than just leaving a note for them saying that their dog has been walked today.'

Abby also takes a canine first-aid course every year and behavioural training courses to ensure that she is always able to offer the dogs the best possible care: 'I was taught that if you are going to do a job, you should do it well. It is just about putting yourself in your client's position and thinking about what you would like someone to do if they were walking your dog.'

Establish a good working relationship

The wonderful thing about working for yourself is that it gives you and your client the freedom to create a working relationship that suits you both.

When Amanda O'Brien began doing some digital marketing consultancy work for University College London, the initial contract was for two days a week for a period of eight weeks. But the university really liked what she was doing and wanted her to continue, so together they were able to come to an arrangement that suited both sides.

Because Amanda travels one week every month to write reviews for her travel blog, the Boutique Adventurer (www.theboutiqueadventurer.com), they agreed that she would work for the university an average of three days per week, but that the actual number of days in any given week could vary considerably, and she could do some of the work either from home or while travelling. But equally, to provide the university with a constant digital marketing presence without them having to pay someone full-time, Amanda agreed that she would manage the campaigns she is running for them every day, regardless of where she is in the world: 'It is a really flexible arrangement and it works really well,' she says. 'If they need me to come in on a particular day one week, for example for a meeting, then I will if I can, and I check in every day to emails and marketing campaigns, no matter where I am, so that I can always respond to something urgent. That way nothing ever gets held up and for the university it is like having a full-time resource.'

Fix the problem

The simplest way to deal with an unhappy client is to offer to fix the problem, regardless of whether it is your fault or theirs that things have gone awry. Offer to redecorate the cake, redo the manicure, repaint the door ... And if you think that you might be at least partly to blame, refund their money too.

If, however, they have already shared their unhappiness online, with a poor review or negative feedback, you have a bigger challenge to address. You also need to reassure your existing and potential customers that all is fine. Reply to the client's original post in a calm, reasonable manner, explain what you are doing to fix the problem – and, if you have genuinely done something wrong, apologise. Depending on the kind of service you offer and the severity of the review, you might also consider contacting any existing customers directly to explain the situation to them yourself.

TOP TIP

Follow up every conversation with a client with an email outlining and confirming what you have both agreed, especially if it is something different from the original plan discussed. This will not only remind you what you are doing, it will provide a permanent record of what was agreed in case of disagreements later.

Chapter 11

Keeping the work coming in

'Don't judge each day by the harvest you reap but by the seeds you plant'

Robert Louis Stevenson, author

Congratulations. Hopefully, by now you've managed to get your first few pieces of work and have succeeded in doing them satisfactorily. Now comes the hard bit: turning that promising start into a fully fledged, ongoing career – one that brings in money, not just this month, but every month.

The way to do this is to start spreading the word about yourself, and the services you offer, to people who might be interested in hiring you, and then to stay in touch with them. It is a crowded market out there, so you can't just sit back and hope that potential clients will somehow magically find you and get in touch. You will have to go out and find them yourself.

In other words, you are going to have to embark on a marketing and communication strategy.

Now, the idea of going around shouting about how brilliant you are can feel rather uncomfortable, particularly if you have been used to being part of a low-key team in a workplace. It can feel a bit like boasting or showing off. Certainly, it would be so much nicer if work could simply show up of its own accord, without you having to go out and hustle for it.

But it isn't going to, so you need to fight the urge to run away and hide. Instead, it's time to start telling the world a bit more about who you are and what you do. And then to make that process an intrinsic part of your weekly routine in order to make the message stick. So here's some advice on how to spread the word.

Start with the right attitude

Your first task is to accept that it is important to do this. It can be tempting to see marketing and promotion as a bit vague and airy-fairy – something that takes you away from doing the work that actually earns you money, and to resent the time you spend on it. A survey by IPSE, representing freelancers and the self-employed, found that many of its members felt that they didn't have time to invest in building and implementing a marketing strategy.

But you need to see marketing and promotion as an intrinsic part of what you do, because it creates a pipeline of future work that will enable you to keep on working for yourself. So set aside some time for it every week and do your best to throw yourself into it with enthusiasm.

Identify the tools at your disposal

Promoting yourself does not just mean attending a networking event and handing out a few business cards while clutching a glass of warm white wine. There are a whole host of tools you can use to draw attention to yourself, both online and offline, many of them free:

- **Email** Use this to send potential clients ideas for their businesses, share interesting articles or even create a newsletter highlighting industry issues of interest.

- **Social media** Share news and photos of an interesting project you have completed, hold a competition or provide special offers and discounts on social media. Depending on your market, this might be on LinkedIn, Twitter, Facebook, Instagram or YouTube.

- **Traditional and online media** This might include national and local newspapers, online or printed magazines and trade publications, online news websites, national and local radio. You could offer to write an article for your local paper or provide some top tips for readers of a relevant magazine.

- **Your own website** Use this to upload videos or write a regular blog on topics of interest to prospective clients.

- **Industry websites** You might contribute guest articles about certain issues to websites relevant to your potential clients.

- **Conferences and industry events** Offer to make a speech or take part in a panel session.

- **Networking** People get scared by the word 'networking', but all it really means is meeting new people and staying in touch with them. There are lots of ways to do this, both face to face and online, including at industry events, networking evenings and through online forums.

- **Testimonials and case studies** If a client likes your work and emails to tell you so, ask them if you can use their kind words as a testimonial on your website and in marketing material, such as leaflets. You could also write up the work you did for them as a case study, explaining what the job called for and how you went about it.

- **Referrals** This is when an existing client recommends you to a potential new one because you have done such fantastic work for them. Referrals can carry an enormous amount of weight because they are genuine endorsements from people who have actually used your services. Encourage clients to recommend you to others by offering them a discount or special reward every time they do so.

Identify the right communication channels

To maximise the impact of your marketing efforts, consider who your potential clients are and therefore the most effective way of telling them you exist: if they live near by, they might read the local newspaper, pick up leaflets or notice posters on noticeboards in the area. Or if they are in the corporate world, they may well be on LinkedIn. Does the market you are targeting have a big presence on Twitter or Facebook or are potential customers more likely to read magazines and check their emails than to go on social media? Are conferences a big deal for your industry – the place where all the key people gather? Or do potential clients tend to network on online forums instead?

The more you can focus your activity in a targeted way, the more likely your efforts are to yield results.

Begin with the people already on board

There is an often-repeated mantra that it is eight times easier to sell something to an existing customer than a new one because they already know and like your business. The same is true when it comes to selling your services. If someone has already worked with you, then assuming that you didn't make a total disaster of it, they are likely to be happy to work with you again because the barriers are already down, the connection has been made and they know they can trust you to do a good job.

So start establishing some kind of regular communication with your existing clients, even if they don't have any work for you, just to remind them that you are there. Don't make the communication about you; make it about them. Email them with suggestions and ideas for future projects, share an interesting photo with them or send them a link to a useful blog you have written.

Show people what you can do

Instead of simply telling potential clients what you can do, show them, so that they'll think it sounds interesting and want you to do it for them too. It's the difference between giving someone a leaflet about how great you are at making furniture and showing them the actual chair.

The good news is that the magic of the Internet makes this easy to do. If you have made a client an amazing dress, ask for their permission to share a picture of it on Instagram. If you have taken a wonderful video of someone's pet, ask if you can put it on your website and then share a link to it on social media.

Initially it might feel rather strange to start promoting your work in this way, particularly if you are used to keeping your head down at work in a large corporate organisation, but it is a great way of showing potential clients what you can do. Get into the habit of doing this regularly, getting permission from the client if needed, and make sure you tag everyone in your post and add a relevant hashtag, so that other people can share it with their followers too.

Be your own brand ambassador

Sarah Jane Moon used to have a full-time job in arts administration, but started working for herself as a portrait painter at the age of 28, having taken a short summer course and realising she loved it.

She took a two-year diploma in portrait painting and now paints full-time at her studio in London, spending half her time working on commissions and the rest on her own creations. She exhibits her work at art galleries around the UK and overseas and also teaches classes at the Heatherley School of Fine Art, where she took her diploma.

Sarah Jane finds clients by constantly creating and cultivating new networks of people that she meets socially. She says: 'My friends jokingly refer to me as Sarah-Jane-have-you-got-my-card-Moon – because everywhere I go, I have a pocket full of business cards. I am quite outgoing and sociable, and I really don't have a problem with going up to someone and telling them who I am and what I do. Then I spend time nurturing these connections, which are social as well as professional, by keeping in touch with people and cultivating networks.'

Sarah Jane also maintains an active presence on social

media: 'I spend at least half an hour a day posting updates on Facebook, Twitter and Instagram about what I am doing, and it really does make a difference. It is how I get most of my commissions. I also send out an email update every two months with news about exhibitions or shows that my work is in.'

She says that the key thing is to keep reminding people that you exist: 'It is important to be in people's minds. Most of the people who commission me and buy my work are people I either know personally or who know somebody who knows me. It is all about cultivating a social scene, keeping in touch with people and having a two-way relationship with them that is based on genuine friendship and mutual interest in each other's lives.'

Stand up and be noticed

No one can give you work if they don't know you are there, so get yourself into the spotlight and start making a bit of noise. The great thing about this method is that if you do it right, people will start approaching you to see if you will work for them, rather than the other way around.

Trade fairs, conferences and other industry events can be a great way of creating a buzz and, in the process, introducing yourself to a large number of potential clients in a relatively short space of time. If you already have considerable expertise in an industry, ask if you can take part in a panel session or even make a short speech. This will give you an ideal opportunity to explain who you are and what you do to an attentive audience. Being on stage will give you added status too. If that is not possible, seek out other ways to get the spotlight on you. Ask interesting questions during Q&A sessions, post pithy comments on social media during the event with the relevant conference hashtags, deliberately sit next to people you don't know at lunch and generally make it your mission to introduce yourself to as many people as you can before the day is over. Even the briefest interactions can make a big impression when done right.

Get into a routine

The secret to promoting yourself successfully is to get into a regular routine of doing it, so that it becomes an intrinsic part of your working day, rather than something you tag on as an afterthought when you are feeling a bit panicky about the lack of work coming in. Consistency is the key because marketing and promotion are cumulative, building on what you have done before. If you start distributing leaflets door to door, don't just do it once – do it every few months, so that people become familiar with the services you are offering. If you are tweeting, make it a rule that you tweet three times a week – for example, on Mondays, Wednesdays and Fridays. If you write a blog, put one up on your website at the same time and day every week or fortnight, so that people come to expect it and start looking out for it. The more you can build your marketing efforts into your regular routine, the more successful they will be.

Trevor Merriden, who helps businesses create content and engage with their customers, has established a highly effective marketing strategy. He spends around 20 per cent of his time every week marketing his services, writing blogs on his website, sharing ideas and content on social media and creating several weekly newsletters which he sends to a network of people who are interested in the services he offers.

He has also identified two hundred potential clients and makes a conscious effort to stay in touch with them personally on a regular basis, emailing them with articles or ideas that they might find interesting. He explains: 'I will send them something fairly systematically every two to three months, such as a relevant article, with a note saying, "I saw this and I thought of you." It might be something that I have written, or it might be something that somebody else has written. It is a way of saying, "Hello, I am still out there." You can't control when the phone is going to ring, but you can try to increase the chances that it will.'

He says that this gentle approach reaps big rewards: 'I never directly ask people for business, but there have been so many times when people have picked up the phone after I have sent something to them and said, "Trevor, I have been meaning to talk to you about an idea." Almost all of my work is picked up through referrals and networks.'

Create a co-ordinated strategy

With so many different ways of promoting yourself and your work, the best results will come if you can link all your activities together because that will stretch whatever you do and make its impact go a lot further.

Every time you add a new photo to your website, for example, also share it on social media. If you are taking part in an event, make sure you also tweet about it at the same time. If you are creating lots of new content, such as blogs and case studies, you could put out a newsletter for potential clients that brings them all together in one place.

But don't be a nuisance

In your enthusiasm to promote yourself, make sure you don't overdo it. No one wants to see your emails popping up in their inbox every five minutes. If your constant communications are annoying someone, you will do more harm than good. Try to achieve a frequency that is regular and consistent, but not overbearing. Make sure too that you comply with legislation – new data protection rules mean that if you want to send out a newsletter, for example, you must first send an email asking people to subscribe to it. You must also include an option for people to unsubscribe from it at any time.

TOP TIP

Start keeping a file of any nice reviews or comments that clients make about you and your work. Even if you don't want to use them immediately as testimonials, they may come in handy later when you want to refresh the look of your website.

———————

Chapter 12

Managing your finances

*'Put all your good eggs in one basket and then watch
that basket'*

Andrew Carnegie, industrialist

When you are an employee with a salaried job you don't have to think too much about how you get paid. Your salary automatically goes into your bank account every month with tax and National Insurance contributions already deducted and your principal job is to decide how to spend it.

When you work for yourself, however, it is a very different experience. You will have to keep track of every piece of work you do and make sure that the client pays you the right amount for it. Then, at the end of the year, you will have to calculate and pay any tax you owe on the money you have earned, plus you may also have to pay VAT (see page 124).

Meanwhile, you must also keep on top of paying for all the utilities and services that you took for granted when you worked for someone else, such as broadband, insurance, mobile phone and printer ink.

Perhaps the biggest issue, though, is that because the amount of work you do is likely to vary from month to month, sometimes substantially, the income you receive may well do the same. This unpredictability is perhaps one of the biggest downsides to working for yourself. Indeed, a survey of freelancers by Moneysupermarket.com found that inconsistent cashflow was the single most annoying thing about working for yourself, with 57.8 per cent of respondents saying that it bothered them.

This means you need to be really good at managing your finances, so that you don't run out of money and find yourself unable to pay a vital bill. HMRC in particular do not look kindly on late payments – they will fine you, and possibly worse.

Here are some key steps to take in order to help you stay on top of your finances and minimise the impact of an erratic income when you start working for yourself:

Create a financial buffer

As we've seen, finding work as a self-employed person can often be unpredictable, particularly when you are starting out – although even when you have been doing it for many years you may still find you hit a drought of several months without work. And getting paid for the work you do can be even more unpredictable, with businesses generally paying invoices at least thirty days after you have completed a project for them, and often far longer.

All of this means that even if you are doing well, you may find yourself going several months with little or no money coming in. So make sure you have a sum of money set aside in a bank account that you can dip into whenever you need to – to pay the bills, to buy essentials and generally tide you over until the money starts flowing in again. Ideally, this sum should be enough to keep you afloat for at least six months.

Of course if you dip into it, you will obviously need to top it up again as soon as you can.

Having enough money to tide you over the lean times does not just enable you to keep going on a practical level and prevent you from having to rush back into a salaried job the moment things go quiet. It also gives you greater comfort and peace of mind, which can enable you to focus on finding and doing good work rather than worrying about how you are going to pay the rent this month.

Marketing consultant and travel blogger Amanda O'Brien explains that before starting to work for herself she'd saved twelve months' salary in a bank account as a financial buffer and now tries to ensure that she maintains this amount as far as she can: 'I knew that I needed that buffer because I would have been way too uncomfortable working for myself without it. I continually top it up. I see it like storing up nuts for winter. I've always taken the view that if that buffer goes down to six months' salary then it is time to stop working for myself and become a full-time marketing director again.'

Set up a separate work bank account

Regardless of whether you are operating as a sole trader or as a limited company, open a dedicated bank account for your work and be strict about keeping it separate from your personal one. Pay everything you earn into your work account and pay out all work-related expenses from there. That way, you will always be able to see precisely how much you have earned from working for yourself, and you will be able to keep track of exactly what is going in and out of your account, and why.

Pay yourself a regular salary

Once you have begun to receive money for the work you do, consider paying yourself a small fixed 'salary' each month – ideally, just enough to cover your mortgage payments or rent, household bills and everyday living expenses – by setting up an automatic transfer from your work account to your personal one. This will provide you with the comfort of a steady – if basic – income each month and smooth the erratic and unpredictable arrival of the actual income coming in. Make sure, however, that you leave enough money in your work account to pay your tax, otherwise you will be in big trouble at the end of the financial year. As a rough guide, basic-rate income tax – which you pay as a sole trader – is currently levied at 20 per cent in the UK, while corporation tax – which you pay as a business – is currently levied at 19 per cent, so you should keep back about a fifth of everything you earn to pay it.

UNDERSTAND VAT

If you think you or your business are likely to earn more than the VAT threshold, currently £85,000 a year, you will need to register for VAT and charge all your clients an additional 20 per cent – the current VAT rate – on top of the fee you have agreed with them. You can register for VAT online at the government website (www.gov.uk) and also complete your VAT returns there. You must pay the VAT you have received from clients in a lump sum to HMRC at the end of every three-month period.

Factor in the lack of holiday and sick pay

When you are in a job you almost take it for granted that you will continue to be paid when you go on holiday or if you are sick and unable to work. So it can come as a real shock when you begin working for yourself to realise that if you go on holiday, you won't earn any money, and if you are too ill to work, you won't earn any money either. It is that simple and that brutal. So if you do go on holiday you not only need to factor in the price of the holiday itself, but also the lost income from all the work you are not doing while you are away. That could mean your holiday is effectively costing you double or even triple the price you paid for it. It is perhaps hardly surprising that people who work for themselves tend not to go on holiday too often. As we will see in Chapter 14, it is still possible to go on holiday when you work for yourself, but you do need to approach it in a different way.

Make time for admin

There is a surprising amount of admin and paperwork that comes with working for yourself. You must not only keep track of the work you have done, for whom and perhaps how long it took if you are being paid by the hour, you must also keep tabs on when you send invoices out, when clients pay you and who owes you money. And that's before you start working out your expenses, your tax and your VAT. So get organised with spreadsheets, cashbooks and software programs to monitor all these things and try to set aside some time each week to ensure that you are staying on top of it. Many self-employed workers set aside Sunday afternoon or evening to deal with admin, so they can start the new week feeling organised and on top of their finances.

Agree payment terms in advance

Before you start doing any work for a client or customer you should agree in advance when and how they are going to pay you. Will they pay you some of the money upfront? Will they pay as soon as you have done the work or will you need to send them an invoice that they will pay at a later date? And will they be paying you in cash, by cheque or by bank transfer, or are they expecting to pay you by debit or credit card?

If you or your business are registered for VAT, you must also make sure they understand that they will need to pay you an additional 20 per cent in VAT on top of the price you have already agreed for the work. It is vital to have this conversation at the outset to avoid misunderstandings later.

If you have agreed to send a client an invoice once you finish the work, make sure you send it to them promptly to avoid any delays in payment. Include your name, address and bank details – account name, account number and sort code – on the invoice, as well as the name, company and company address of the person you are invoicing. If you are a registered business, include your company registration number, and if you are registered for VAT include your VAT number too.

At the bottom of the invoice you should add a sentence requesting that you are paid within a certain number of days of receipt of the invoice – thirty days is the recognised standard payment terms for a business.

If you are likely to be doing more work for the same client, they might decide to set you up in their payments system, so keep an eye out for any emails requesting bank and address details and call them to check it is genuine if you have any concerns.

Chase outstanding payments

If you don't receive your money within thirty days plus one week of sending your invoice, get in touch with the client, or with their accounts department if they have one, to check that your invoice is being processed. If it isn't, find out why – it could be that you haven't provided enough information or followed procedure correctly – and when it is likely to be paid. Once you have chased them and provided any missing details give them a few more weeks to pay, and if they continue not to pay, stay on the case. Phone them in person, using your best no-nonsense voice, as emails are too easy to ignore. Then phone again the following week. That will often do the trick.

If that still doesn't produce payment, for a small fee – typically less than £5 – you can instruct a solicitor to send your client a formal letter known as a 'Letter Before Action'. This will ask them to pay up within a set time period – typically seven days – and warn that you will apply to the County Court to claim the money you are owed if they do not pay up. You are entitled to add interest and compensation to the outstanding amount.

If that doesn't work either, you can use a mediation service to try and reach agreement – details of how to do this can be found on the government website (www.gov.uk) or you can make a claim online through the same website for outstanding amounts of up to £100,000. You will need to pay a small fee. The claim will be sent to the person or business that owes you money and they will need to respond by a specified date. If they still don't pay up, you can ask the County Court to order them to pay. For the sake of your future working relationship, however, you should try to resolve the situation before it gets to this point.

Luis Costa, the freelance photographer, is forever having to chase unpaid invoices. He says: 'It is always a struggle to get paid on time because although clients like to receive the pictures really fast, they don't like to pay fast. I currently have four invoices which have not been paid and two of them are several months late. My terms of payment are fifteen days, but nobody ever pays on time.

Luis usually deals with the problem by ringing the client direct. He says: 'I have good relationships with my clients, so most of the time I don't have to chase the accounts departments – I just call my clients and say, "Look, I haven't been paid yet. What is going on? Can you check that for me?"'

He explains that it is important to try to chase payments in such a way that doesn't damage your relationship with the client: 'It is a fine line – you have to chase payments when you work for yourself because nobody is going to do it for you, but you also don't want to put people off. When you get to the point where you have to call every day, that's bad news because it means your relationship with the client is not great. So I chase periodically. If the payment is really running late, then you have to be a bit more persistent, but try to give them some space to breathe as well as chasing them, otherwise you risk losing a client.'

Factor in your costs

Depending on the kind of service you are offering, you may have some overheads that you cannot pass on to the client, which you must pay out of any income you receive. For example, an alternative health and wellbeing practitioner will have to pay to rent a therapy room, while a handyman will have to pay the cost and upkeep of a van and tools.

These expenses will come straight out of your income, so do your sums carefully to make sure you are getting the best deal and, most importantly, that you can still make a profit from what you are doing. If, say, it is costing you £400 a month to rent a room to provide reflexology sessions to clients, but you are only managing to take £800 a month in fees, you need to ask yourself whether you might be better off changing your model so that you provide reflexology treatments in people's homes instead, for example.

Get an accountant

Filing your annual tax return and company accounts can be extremely time-consuming if you don't know what you are doing – and even if you do. And that's before you've got started on calculating your expenses and filing your VAT return online. The good news is that you don't have to tear your hair out trying to make the numbers add up – you can hire an accountant to do it all for you instead. Choose a local firm of accountants who have been recommended to you and agree a fee before you proceed. Yes, it will cost you a few hundred pounds each year (more if your business is complex), but it will be worth it, not just in terms of the time and effort saved, but also because you won't have to worry about whether you added up the figures correctly or not. You can even include the fee as an expense in your accounts the following year.

Alex Mallinson, who works for himself creating digital animations, got so caught up in the demands of working for himself that for the first five years he failed to submit a tax return or pay any tax. It was not a good idea.

He says: 'I wish I had known to get an accountant because I massively screwed up right at the start. I missed the deadline for doing my tax return in the first year and so didn't pay any tax, and then somehow, I just got into a cycle of doing that and missed several years. I told myself that I was a creative, and so I should just do the creative stuff. But I was in a panic. I had sleepless nights. I was absolutely living in terror; I was running away from it and just not facing up to it.'

Eventually Alex realised that he needed help. He initially went to see a tax advisor who reassured him that it could be sorted out, so he hired an accountant. The accountant calculated that Alex owed several thousand pounds in taxes, fines and interest. Alex did not have enough money to pay this, but fortunately HMRC agreed to let him pay off the amount he owed in instalments over several months.

It all took a tremendous toll on him, however: 'The stress of it meant that I lost work because I just couldn't focus enough to be able to do any work. When I agreed the payment plan with HMRC I worked really hard to make the payments because I hated the idea of being in debt.'

Alex has now learned his lesson, saying: 'At the start of April every year I jump on the computer and download my entire bank account into a spreadsheet and drag numbers across columns. There is a joy in doing it because I know what the alternative is.'

Know the rules and regulations

If you have set up a limited company, it is important to be aware that HMRC is increasingly clamping down on situations that it does not regard as being genuine self-employment, with legislation called IR35.

This is because although most of the differences have been eroded away, there are still some small tax advantages to being set up as a business rather than a sole trader. If you are employed by your own business you only pay tax on your income when you actually withdraw it from your company; you can pay for work expenses out of your pre-tax income; and you can choose to take part of your income as a dividend rather than as a salary, which reduces or eliminates the amount of National Insurance contributions you make.

HMRC is particularly keen to crack down on situations where people appear to all intents and purposes to be doing the job of an employee and yet are paid via their own businesses, sometimes referred to as personal service companies, purely to avoid tax. While it is fairly obvious that someone is genuinely self-employed if they work from home doing projects for lots of different clients, it becomes less easy to determine in situations where someone works full-time in a client's office doing the same job for several months or even years. To make matters more complicated, there is no legal definition of what being 'self-employed' means, so each case has to be assessed on an individual basis.

HMRC bases its decision on any contracts you may have signed with clients, but will also look at the nature of the working relationship in practice, in case it differs from what is written in the contract.

If you are investigated by the HMRC and it concludes that

you are an employee and not self-employed, you will have to pay any additional tax and National Insurance contributions owed plus interest, and if they decide that you have deliberately flouted the rules you will be charged a penalty too.

If you are at all concerned about whether the way you work could put you within IR35 legislation you can do one or all of these:

1. Consult your accountant or a tax advisor who specialises in IR35.

2. Use the HMRC's online IR35 employment status checker. Search for 'Check Employment Status for Tax' on the gov. uk website. The service is free and anonymous. If you still aren't sure whether the rules apply to your situation, you can contact the IR35 helpline either by email on ir35@ hmrc.gov.uk or by phone on 0300 123 2326. HMRC states that you don't need to reveal your identity to use the helpline and any information you do give will not be shared with HMRC compliance teams.

3. Get a tax advisor to review any written contracts you have entered into with clients to determine whether the IR35 legislation applies to them. HMRC also provides a free online contract checker service on the gov.uk website.

4. Buy tax investigations insurance. This covers you for the cost of dealing with a tax investigation, in particular paying for the services of an accountant or specialist tax advisor.

TOP TIP

Always carry your work account debit card with you so that you can use it to pay for any work expenses instead of putting them on your personal debit card and then having to transfer the money. It will make your accounts much easier to understand.

Chapter 13

Adjusting to working independently

'It is far better to be alone than to be in bad company'

George Washington, American president

One of the most exciting aspects of working for yourself is the freedom and independence it gives you, not just in terms of the kind of work you do, but also how you actually do it.

Instead of having a boss or line manager constantly barking instructions or peering over your shoulder, now that you work for yourself you are free to tackle a piece of work in any way you choose. There is also no one to frown at you if you hum while you work or get up to make a cup of tea every half an hour, and no one to complain that you are hogging the printer.

This sense of freedom can feel exciting and liberating, but it might also initially feel a little daunting. Here are some strategies for dealing with the transition.

Take it slowly

If you are used to working in a lively workplace surrounded by the constant buzz and chatter of other employees, it can be a bit of a shock to swap that for the silence of your empty home. Even if you have been dreaming of doing this for years, the reality can still take some getting used to. To begin with, you may even find yourself putting the radio on simply to hear someone talking.

Even if you have chosen to work in a co-working space or shared office, rather than at home, it can still feel quite odd, because everyone else around you will be doing different kinds of work for different clients and so won't be interrupting you in the way that colleagues would, to ask for your advice or catch up on the latest gossip.

So don't panic, give yourself time to adjust, enjoy the sensation of working in a completely different way and make the most of being able to complete a task or email in one go without someone demanding your attention.

Discover your own way of doing things

Large businesses and organisations often have their own set processes for carrying out the work they do, sometimes for no better reason than that is the way it has always been done. For employees, it can often be immensely frustrating to have to do things in a particular way, especially if they can see that there is a far better way of doing it.

Well, here's the good news. You don't have to do that any-more. Now that you work for yourself, you can create your own processes and procedures and do things in a way that makes more sense to you. You can start a job from the middle or the end, lay it out any way you choose and tackle it in the order that you decide. Not only will it make you feel happier and more in control, you may find that your clients appreciate your fresh perspective too.

Step up to the responsibility

When you work for an employer as part of a team, there is safety in numbers. If something goes wrong, there is always a system failure to blame, a boss to take responsibility or someone else to share the fallout with.

When you work for yourself, however, there is nowhere to hide. You, and you alone, are responsible for the work you do. It's a scary thought at first, but it also gives you immense power to show the world what you are capable of. If it is a disaster you take all the blame, but equally, if it is a success then you take all the glory.

Cultivate sources of specialist advice

When you work for a business or organisation as an employee and you come across an aspect of the job that you cannot do, you are likely to have colleagues or managers you can ask for advice. But when you work for yourself you may not have anyone to ask. If it is a query about the project you are working on, you can obviously ask the client, but if it's a query about the service you are offering – that you are supposed to be an expert in – they are not going to be very impressed if you confess that you have no idea what you are doing.

Therefore, you need to create your own hotline of expert

advice that you can tap into whenever you need to. Depending on the kind of services you are offering, you might be able to find this through your industry members association, through other people you know who work in the same industry, through other freelance friends or even online.

Create a diversion

If you enjoy working alone, but find that you miss the camaraderie of being in an office or workplace, consider forming a local group of people who also work for themselves. The fantastic thing about the growth in self-employment is that you are unlikely to be the only one working this way in your area. Many towns that would have once shut down during the day as people commuted to work elsewhere are now a buzz of activity during working hours as people who work for themselves fill cafés, leisure centres and parks.

Put up a notice in your local café or library inviting other freelancers to get in touch, or post an invitation on Meetup (www.meetup.com) which enables you to set up a group for free. If you find you get on well, then consider making it a regular event. You could also check out Jelly (www.uk-jelly.org.uk), an informal co-working event for people who work for themselves, to see if there is already a group in your area.

Katy Carlisle works for herself as a website developer. She creates websites for freelancers and charities, using the website tool Squarespace, and runs workshops to teach other people how to create websites for themselves.

When she first started working for herself, having previously had full-time salaried jobs as a teacher and then with a charity, she loved the freedom and independence it gave her. But after six months of working alone at her home in the Peak District, she realised she was becoming lonely and isolated: 'When I first started, I was really looking forward to working from home, just me and my computer, but after about six months, I realised that I needed to talk to people. I didn't want to commit to a full co-working space, so I went to some cafés to see if I could chat to anybody there. But people were all very focused on their own work. I thought about putting up a little sign on my table saying, "If you are another freelancer and want to chat, come and join me." But I was worried about attracting the wrong kind of people.'

So in 2015 Katy started up a freelance community called Freelance Folk, an informal group of people who meet every Friday afternoon in a café in Manchester. Between ten and twenty freelance professionals, including copywriters, illustrators, artists, designers and life coaches, turn up each week to work alongside each other, share issues and make connections.

Katy is now looking at new ways to bring people who work for themselves together, including a freelancer directory and a scheme for venues to host their own Freelance Folk events across the country. She runs the group entirely on a voluntary basis and in 2017 won the IPSE Ambassador of the Year award for her work supporting the freelance community.

Be a magpie

If you like working on your own, but fancy the occasional dose of office life, investigate whether you might be able to work in your clients' offices, perhaps one day a week at a spare desk. The added bonus of this arrangement is that by being a regular presence in their workplace, you will be a constant reminder to them that you exist and are available for work, so you may pick up additional projects.

Schedule face-to-face meetings

If you find that you are spending too much time alone with your computer or work tools, arrange some face-to-face meetings or coffee catch-ups with someone you know who works in the same field. It can be really good to have the opportunity to talk generally about your industry and what is going on, and even if these conversations don't lead directly to any work, they may provide fresh ideas and new perspectives. Talking on the phone is no substitute for the insights, nuances and humour that can arise when you meet someone in person. So every month, look at your diary and book in some meet-ups.

If you need to travel some distance to a large town or city to meet someone, consider scheduling several back-to-back meetings on the same day in the same place to save on time and transport costs. It can also be surprisingly inspiring having a whole day discussing ideas with people.

Find a work partner

If you miss being able to bounce ideas off work colleagues, then depending on the type of services you offer, you could consider finding a partner who can work alongside you doing the same sort of thing as you. That could be an option if you are an illustrator, virtual PA or accountant, for example. Because you are both in the same field of work there will be endless opportunities to brainstorm ideas and discuss opportunities. And there may be other advantages to simply having someone to share your working day with; if they have skills which complement and add to your own, the two of you working together may be able to take on a much wider range of projects than you could have on your own.

Seek out other people like you

Even if you don't want a work partner, it can still be beneficial to meet up with people who work in the same field as you on a regular basis. Not only can it give you a real sense of being part of a community, you may also pick up useful tips and contacts.

Stoney Parsons is a stained-glass artist who works to commission making stained-glass doors and panels for restaurants and other buildings, including a screen and pillar for Raymond Blanc's Michelin-starred restaurant Le Manoir Aux Quat'Saisons, near Oxford. She works in her studio near her home in Tunbridge Wells and is a member of the Chelsea Arts Club in London. She now travels up there once a week to chat to other artists and play snooker. She says, 'I love my work and when I am doing an intense piece of work I don't need anyone around, but I definitely get lonely sometimes. If you work in an office, there is always a bit of banter and people to make you laugh if you are feeling a bit down, and I think not having that is one of the biggest downsides to working for yourself. I listen to Radio 4 when I am working but I realised that I needed people to talk to, so I joined the Chelsea Arts Club to be around like-minded people. And it really does work. There are a lot of artists there and they all have the same issues about their work, so there is that commonality, which is really meaningful. It is helpful to know that other people are in the same boat.'

Stoney also started teaching art classes once a month in her studio, calling them Art from the Heart, and now every summer she also teaches art classes for several weeks at Skyros, a creative retreat which has centres on the Greek island of Skyros and on the Isle of Wight. 'I am quite a gregarious person and I like being able to share what is in my head with other people,' she says. 'When you work for yourself it can be easy to forget the self-care bit, but that is really important. We are human beings, not machines.'

Build watercooler moments into your day

If you find that you love working alone, but miss having people to pass the time of day with, you could always check out the neighbours.

Jacqueline Cloake is a freelance voice-over artist and narrator who does voice-overs for television and radio adverts and documentaries, getting work through an agent. She lives in a small house in London during the week to be close to recording studios, and in an apartment in Somerset at weekends, and in both places she has deliberately taken the time to get to know her neighbours, so that she always has someone to have a conversation with: 'In London I live in a gated community and in Somerset I live in a converted country house, so there is always someone around for a chat and a cup of tea,' she explains. 'Having that sense of community is so important to me and it means I never get lonely.'

Jacqueline also makes the most of her agent's office. She says: 'My agent has a recording studio at their office which is great because when I'm there I'll often bump into other voice-over artists. Everybody is always friendly and it's like one big family. Even if I am not recording at the agency, I will often pop in to say hi.'

Build a regular event into your week

You could join a local softball team that meets after work one day a week to play a game in the park, volunteer for a couple of hours per week in your local charity shop, or even work a lunchtime shift in your local pub once a week. Simply being around other people for a short sharp blast of conviviality can be amazingly therapeutic.

TOP TIP

Follow the sun. The single best thing about working for yourself is being able to suddenly drop everything for an hour or so when the sun comes out, to bask outside in the garden or park. That simple act of blissful freedom is usually not possible when you work for someone else on their time schedule, and will remind you why you made the move.

———————

Chapter 14

How to manage your work–life balance

'Never get so busy making a living that you forget to make a life'

Dolly Parton, singer-songwriter

One of the trickiest aspects about working for yourself is trying not to let it engulf all the other parts of your life, such as your partner, children, friends, hobbies or sporting activities.

This can be a particular challenge if you work from home, but it can affect anyone who is self-employed. The problem is that because your income stream relies entirely on you ensuring that work keeps flowing in, it can be really hard to switch off.

However, you do need to make the effort because otherwise you will eventually wear yourself out and collapse in a heap.

Make time for friends and family

One of the biggest casualties of your decision to start working for yourself is likely to be the time you used to spend with friends and family. When you were in a salaried position your evenings and weekends may have been spent relaxing in their company and thinking of anything but your job, whereas when you work for yourself it is really hard to forget about what you do, because your waking hours are filled with the constant buzz of your phone as emails arrive in your inbox and clients phone you with queries and concerns. One rogue email that urgently needs a detailed and considered response can be all it takes to ruin an evening or social event, and your friends and family may quickly tire of you leaving the table muttering, 'I just need to do this ... it won't take long, I promise.'

You need to consciously carve out time to spend with them, and them alone, without the constant and unwelcome ghostly presence of your clients in the room. So set aside a specific client-resistant time to be with them, such as Saturday morning or Sunday afternoon. Then try to make sure that when you actually are with your loved ones, you are fully focused on being with them. Put your phone in your pocket on silent and block the urge to check your emails every five minutes.

Make time for sport and exercise

Sport and exercise provide the perfect balance to working for yourself because they force you to switch off. When you are going for a run, swimming or playing football you can't answer your phone and you can't write an email, bake, create, build – or whatever your work involves. Even better, sport and exercise deliver all kinds of benefits that you need when you work for yourself: fresh air to give you an oxygen boost, mood-boosting endorphins to make you feel alive and happy, strenuous physical effort to ensure that you get a good night's sleep and nothing particular to focus on, to enable you to free your mind to think about new projects and ideas.

Even better, if you work from home you may be able to do your sport activity and exercise during the day, meaning that you get the double benefit of an uncrowded gym and possibly off-peak prices. Try to build some regular exercise into your routine every day.

Embrace the freedom that working for yourself can deliver

One of the best things about working for yourself is the freedom to set your own schedule – and then to change it whenever you feel like it too. So make the most of it, otherwise you might as well still be in a nine-to-five job.

Andrew Stone has been a freelance business journalist for twenty years, writing articles for newspapers, as well as content and reports for organisations. He lives in Brighton with his fiancée and baby. 'I love almost everything about being a freelancer,' he says. 'I love having the freedom to move around, I don't have to do a commute and I get to exercise when I want. I can even put my laptop in my rucksack and go walking for a day and work on the road. It also means that I get to spend lots of time with my young son and it is a great privilege to be able to do that. I feel very lucky to be able to do what I do. Compared to having a job, it feels like I am winning.'

Make time for holidays

There is no escaping the fact that going away on holiday can be hard to do when you work for yourself. First, because it can be really difficult to schedule a break between projects in advance in order to be able to book some time off. And second, because when you work for yourself you don't get paid holiday leave. So it's a double whammy of financial pain if you do manage to get away because you will effectively be paying for your holiday twice – once for the actual cost of the holiday, and once for the lost income while you are away.

But despite the challenges, it is incredibly important to have a break every now and then to recharge your batteries, because otherwise you will simply burn out. Also, if you were planning on breaking the news to your partner or children that they aren't going to be able to go on holiday anymore now that you've started working for yourself, good luck with that. So holidays it is.

Here's how to do it in the least disruptive way:

Time it right

Most industries have a quiet time of year when very little happens, so once you have been working for yourself for a while, look back through your notebook where hopefully you have been writing down all your work commissions and try to get a sense of when that quiet time occurs. If you organise weddings, for example, you are likely to find that January is generally pretty quiet, while August is hectic; if you work for financial-services firms it will be the other way around. If you can go on holiday in the quiet times, you are less likely to miss out on work – and you will sharply reduce the likelihood of work being unexpectedly sprung on you at the last minute, disrupting your holiday.

Manage expectations

If the service you offer can only be done by you in person or in a particular location – cutting someone's hair, for example, or tiling their bathroom – then you should tell your clients well in advance that you are going away on holiday, so that they have time to book you in before you leave, or know that they will have to wait until you get back. Be prepared to work a lot of extra hours in the run-up to your holiday in order to fit everyone in.

Be contactable

If the kind of work you do requires you to answer questions or offer advice once you have completed a project, reassure your clients that they will still be able to contact you while you are away, tell them how best to get in touch and make sure that you check your phone, emails or social media regularly while you are on holiday.

Take it with you

If your work is mainly phone- or computer-based, you may be able to take some of it with you. This is not ideal because you won't really be getting a break from work at all – but on the plus side, it will enable you to maintain a continuous service for your clients and stop them leaving you to go off to a competitor. It will also enable you to keep earning at least some money while you are away. Here's how to do it:

- **Accept the limitations** It may not be ideal trying to squeeze your work into small pockets of available time early in the morning and late at night, and you may have to miss the odd museum or trip to the beach. However, you do at least get a change of view, the chance for a dip in the pool in between work activity, the odd meal out in a local restaurant and, hopefully, a bit of sun. So there's that.

- **Make sure you book somewhere with efficient Wi-Fi** Forget the amazing view – the only thing that really matters to you is that the hotel, campsite or resort where you are staying has strong, reliable Wi-Fi everywhere, preferably free. Otherwise you will be barrelling through your mobile data allowance in a seriously painful way.

- **Take lots of travel plug adaptors** ... then pack some more. You will be amazed how many you need, once you factor in all the things you need to charge up, and how many the rest of your family are going to borrow from you.

- **Stick to a similar time zone** If you have to speak to clients while you are away, it is going to be a lot easier if you don't have to get up at 3a.m. to do it. Choose a holiday destination that's on the same time zone as home or no more than a couple of hours ahead or behind. This will also prevent the risk that you will be jetlagged and talking nonsense on conference calls.

- **Don't go too far away** If there is any chance at all that you will have to come home early to sort out an unexpected work problem, go somewhere you can either drive or get the train to, or which is only a couple of hours away by plane. Check too the frequency of the flights home – if there are only a couple of flights a week, then rule it out.

- **Remember the upside** Trying to have a holiday while working for yourself is never going to be easy, but when your friends are back at work in their nine-to-five jobs after their annual two weeks away in Majorca with nothing but a fading tan and some Facebook photos to show for it, you can still go for walks in the park, enjoy a daily swim, meet friends for lunch and generally structure your working day exactly as you please. And the benefits of that will last all year round.

Make time for adventures

One of the lovely things about working for yourself is that you don't have to give up your job to have an adventure. No more trying to persuade the boss to give you three weeks off in one go or wondering whether it is worth trying to negotiate some unpaid time off and hoping that your job will still be there when you get back. This way *you* get to set the rules. So make sure you do.

Simon Foster works for himself managing IT projects for clients, but in 2018 he took eight weeks off to join the Clipper Round the World Yacht race for a leg, sailing from Seattle to New York. During the two years leading up to the race he took five weeks off for training at sea and also trained on land in his spare time. 'I would never have been able to take part in the race if I had been an employee in a salaried job because I wouldn't have been able to take the time off,' says Simon. 'A lot of people who took part in the race had to quit their jobs to do it. It has been so much easier doing it this way. I just had to make sure that I didn't take on any work for the time I knew I was going to be away doing the race, and then I simply got more work when I got back – although it took a month or so to find a good project.'

TOP TIP

Get into the habit of being able to go away at short notice when a gap in your work schedule appears. Keep your passport and driving licence to hand (and up to date), always have the necessary travel adaptors and a travel bag for your computer, and your travel insurance organised and you are good to go. Even a couple of nights away can be a real tonic.

Chapter 15

Managing the unpredictability

*'Never let the fear of striking out keep you from
playing the game'*

Babe Ruth, baseball player

Perhaps the biggest single reason why more people don't take the leap into working for themselves is the amount of unpredictability involved – the uncertainty of wondering where the next piece of work is going to come from, and the fear of not making enough money to pay the bills.

It is certainly an important aspect to take on board. Although salaried jobs don't come with any long-term guarantees either, many self-employed people literally move from one piece of work – which could last anything from an hour to a few weeks – to the next, with no guarantee that any more work will appear once it is done. Even working on a fixed-term contract, perhaps as an independent IT contractor, will only guarantee you work for several months. This means that even the most successful self-employed workers are occasionally gripped by the fear that the work will suddenly grind to a halt.

However, the good news is that you can take active steps to reduce the fear and insecurity of working for yourself. Here's how to go about it.

Create several income streams

The great thing about working for yourself is that you don't have to limit yourself to one way of making money. Indeed, the most successful people who work for themselves have a range of different services they can offer. This is sometimes known as having a portfolio career. If you make dresses, for example, you could also consider offering private sewing lessons or running dressmaking workshops, so that when one source of income hits a lull you can still continue to make money from one of the others.

This is particularly important if the work you want to do is seasonal. If you are a water-sports instructor, for example, you will be very busy in the summer months, but will need to find another skill to offer during the winter months, perhaps as a ski guide.

Ideally, you should also never rely on one single client for all your work, no matter how big they are. Even if you have lots of work coming in from them, it makes sense to continue to pitch for work from other clients as a back-up, even if it means that you occasionally have more work than you need. This way, if your big client unexpectedly dumps you, you will still have something else to keep you afloat.

At the start of 2018, Oliver Webb, who works for himself selling advertising space in medical journals, found himself with some free time. So he decided to take a training course to become a drone pilot to give himself another skill he could offer clients if the advertising work fell off. He now holds a

Permission for Commercial Operations and gets work taking aerial pictures of building projects and filming motor racing events from the sky.

Oliver says: 'It appealed to me because it is a reasonably well-regulated area that will become more regulated and I thought that if I got on board now it could become something slightly larger in the future. It is a side gig that gives me something new to think about and I am starting to make money from it.'

Try to establish recurring income

Repeat or recurring income is a wonderful thing when you work for yourself because it means you already know you will be receiving a certain income every month without having to go out and pitch for it. Services that involve teaching or maintaining things – music lessons, French tuition and garden services, for example – are ideal candidates for this, as clients already appreciate that they will need to hire your services over and over again, say, every week or every month, in order to achieve the maximum benefit from them.

But whatever kind of service you offer, it is still worth considering whether it could be turned into a regular engagement which brings in recurring income, perhaps by offering a customer the incentive of a small discount if they agree to sign up for a certain number of sessions. Arranging to clean clients' windows once a month or to dye their hair every six weeks, for example, can give you a nice regular core income which will go a long way to reducing the unpredictability of your earnings.

Keep your skills up to date

Make sure you keep your skills fresh and relevant by going on training courses and staying informed about developments in your industry. When you work for an employer in a job, they may take charge of this as part of your career development, and pay for it too. When you work for yourself, however, all this is down to you.

It can be tempting to let this slide, particularly because attending a course takes you away from doing paid work and it can be expensive. But it is important that you continually invest in your professional training and development, not just to update the skills you have, but to ensure that you adhere to the best-practice standards in the industry and incorporate the newest ways of doing things. Otherwise your knowledge and skills will become irrelevant and out of date, and so will you.

According to an Upwork survey of US freelancers in 2017, people who work for themselves are nearly twice as likely as salaried employees to proactively take on reskilling themselves, which means that even if you are not doing it, your competitors almost certainly are.

Robyn Elliot is an independent social worker who started working for herself after being employed by her local authority for fifteen years. Much of her work consists of conducting assessments for solicitors, local authorities and adoption and fostering charities on projects that typically last three months. She works partly from her home in Edinburgh and partly from a nearby co-working space.

Robyn regularly undertakes professional training courses to stay on top of the demands of her profession, including a five-day full-time accredited course in Theraplay, a child and family therapy, and a four-day distance learning course in mediation training. She had to pay for both courses herself, each at a cost of around £1000. She also does lots of free one-day courses provided by the professional bodies and organisations that represent the social-work profession.

All of this takes commitment. Robyn says: 'I have to think carefully before I take a course and make sure that this is something that is going to be of benefit to me. I am also always on the lookout for free courses provided by regulatory bodies.' However, she knows how important it is to keep up to date with her training, particularly as she now has a much more varied workload than she did when she worked for her local authority: 'It is really important for anybody, but it is particularly important in the social-work profession that you keep on the ball with experience and training and that you are up to date with new things that are being said.'

Ensure that your home is fit for purpose

One of the most important pieces of the jigsaw to get right is to ensure that you have a secure base from which to work.

If you rent your property and plan to work from home, check your tenancy agreement to make sure there are no exclusion clauses preventing you from doing this, particularly if you are living in a council property or social housing. If you are allowed to work from home, but prohibited in the agreement from using it as a formal business address, consider renting a virtual business address instead (see page 70). You can use this on invoices and work correspondence and any post sent to the virtual address will be forwarded on to you. Firms such as Regus offer this service. Alternatively, you could ask your accountant if you can use their address.

Note that if your work involves preparing food, your

kitchen may need to conform to certain health-and-safety standards and be inspected by your local council in order to be granted a permit. Check their website for details.

Perhaps the most important thing for anyone working from home is to have fast, reliable broadband and good mobile phone coverage. If potential clients can't get hold of you to offer you work, or to check on progress, you are going to be in big trouble. The quality and availability of both broadband and mobile phone reception can differ markedly around the country, with some rural areas having neither, so check out your area using an online broadband speed checker guide, such as the free one provided by the consumer guide site Which (www.which.co.uk).

Secure your finances

While you are building up your income stream, only spend what you absolutely need to on living costs, set aside enough money to pay your tax and VAT and keep topping up your financial buffer (see page 122) so that you have something to keep you afloat when work is scarce.

Don't panic . . .

There is a huge amount of freelance work out there and it is growing as more and more businesses realise that it makes sense to hire skilled, flexible self-employed workers for specific projects, as and when they need them. It may take you a while to find the work, and you may have to step up your marketing efforts and tweak the services you can offer to fit the needs of clients, but it is out there.

... but don't ever become complacent

Projects and clients can disappear without warning, even if you have been doing work for them for many years. No matter how good your work is, or how much your client values you, no one is indispensable when times are tough and budgets are cut.

Andrew Stone has been a freelance business journalist for twenty years and loves what he does. It hasn't stopped him from experiencing the fragility of being self-employed, however: 'I had this absolutely shocking eighteen months in 2009 and 2010, where all the projects I had lined up fell over, the phone stopped ringing and the emails stopped pinging in. I had got quite complacent and had a really tough time. For three or four months, I found it hard to motivate myself to find new work and worried much of the time about paying the bills. It wasn't a great place to be and having just moved to a new town, I didn't have a network of other freelancers near by, and I didn't have a partner to confide in or support me emotionally or financially. I had to cold-call people to look for new clients, which I don't enjoy and am not that good at, and I had to rent out every room in my house to lodgers.' After eighteen months of cold-calling, work gradually began to trickle back in, but it was a stark reminder that the freedom of working for yourself can sometimes come at a price. 'One of the downsides to being a freelancer is the insecurity of it. You have to accept that, and you have to be a bit paranoid. You can never be comfortable. No one owes you a living. If you think you haven't got enough clients, you just have to hit the phone.'

Spot the warning signs

It is wonderful having a regular customer or client who consistently pops up to give you more work. And it can come as a really unpleasant shock if they suddenly drop you out of the blue. Fortunately, there are often some tell-tale indications that all might not be well, and it can be useful to know what they are:

1. The client displays a sudden surge of interest in the work you are doing and how you are doing it. On the face of it, this may seem like a positive thing, but in reality, their interest could be in checking out whether you are really worth the money they are paying you. If you have always been left alone to get on with work, whether it is photographing a scene or tutoring their child, and out of the blue the client asks to accompany you to the photography shoot or sit in on the lesson, that can be bad news.

2. The client asks you to do the work in a different way. If you have always gone about building cyber-security systems or making videos for them in a certain way, and they decide they want you to change your approach, this could be a sign that they are restless with the current arrangement and are considering making changes.

3. Your long-standing project is taken over by new people you don't have a personal relationship with. New staff coming into a project within an organisation generally like to assert their authority and show that they are in charge by making changes, sometimes just for the sake of it.

4. They start paying you late. If they have been good about paying you on time so far, this could be a sign that you

are less important to them than you were and that they no longer care about maintaining a good relationship with you.

5. The client constantly changes their mind about what they want and how they want you to do it. This is never a good sign because it indicates either that the project is no longer a top priority for them, so may be canned, or that someone else higher up the organisation is now in control of it and your contact no longer has the power to make decisions.

6. Being invited in to discuss how the project you are working on can be expanded can trip you up, as has happened to me several times. Confusingly, clients often embark on this sort of conversation just before they pull the plug on the whole venture. This is because they are trying to find ways of keeping a doomed project alive, and when they realise that isn't going to work, they ditch the whole thing.

7. The client starts rejecting all the ideas you put forward. This is a rather demoralising but extremely effective way for a client to get rid of you because it shifts the blame for the work drying up onto you and your inability to inspire them enough to want to commission you.

Accept that it will be a roller-coaster ride

Sometimes you will have so much work flowing in you won't know what to do with yourself; other times you will be scraping the barrel. Sometimes you will be able to plan ahead with work scheduled in advance; other times work will show up without any warning. And there is no easy way of controlling any of this. The best thing to do is to just accept that this unpredictability is an unavoidable part of working for yourself. It comes with the territory. So take a deep breath and remember that the flip side of unpredictability is freedom and all the other wonderful advantages that come with working for yourself.

TOP TIP

Make a point of ending every work arrangement on good terms, even if you are seething with fury or disappointment inside. Remember that people can change jobs, and that their personal circumstances can change, so that client who is pulling the plug on your project today could pop up in a completely different context in a year's time and get in touch to offer you work. Make sure that they remember you in a positive light.

———————

Chapter 16

When there's too much work

'Life has many ways of testing a person's will,
either by having nothing happen at all or by having
everything happen all at once'

Paulo Coelho, author

When Ronan Keating sang 'Life is a Rollercoaster' he might well have been singing about working for yourself. One minute you are staring at a blank calendar with a knot in your stomach, wondering if you will ever earn any money again, the next you have so much work and so little time in which to do it that you wonder if you will ever sleep again.

On the face of it, having too much work sounds like the ultimate dream for someone who is self-employed – a welcome respite from the drudgery of pitching for commissions, the warming ego-boost of knowing that your services are in demand, the excitement of having interesting work to get stuck into, a happy break from worrying about how to pay the bills. What's not to love?

In reality, however, it is anything but. That's because

what would have been a joyful project to work on in a calm, thoughtful way, quickly becomes the project from hell when squeezed in between three equally demanding ones, all requiring your attention at the same time.

The problem is that as a self-employed worker, it just doesn't feel right turning down work, no matter how overburdened you are. That's because you would be not only saying no to the job on offer, you might also be saying no to all the other work that it could have led to: the painting job that could have led to a house renovation, the feature that could have led to a regular column, the birthday cake that could have led to catering for a three-day wedding. What's more, deep down, you strongly suspect that the minute you say no to anything, your entire workload will instantly dry up and no one will ever offer you any work again.

Melvin Boughtwood is a self-employed gardener in Great Abington, Cambridge. He provides garden maintenance services in the summer and painting services in the winter months. He started working for himself at the age of 54, having worked for many years as a manager of an agricultural business.

He started out with two days of work a week already lined up and since then his workload has grown rapidly, as more and more customers have decided they would like him to look after their gardens too. After just six months Melvin was booked up solidly and since then has always had too much work: 'Everybody thinks that when working for yourself it is going to be a struggle to get work, but when the opposite happens, it is hard to know how to control it. I shouldn't complain about it, but it can be very stressful because there are only so many hours in the day and it is quite a physical job as well. It is my own fault for taking jobs on that I don't really have time to do, but sometimes it is very difficult to say no to people if they are standing in front of you, because you want to help them and you know that they will appreciate it.'

Melvin is now working far longer hours than he had planned to, as well as Saturday mornings, and he didn't take any time off at all last year apart from a week at Christmas. Part of the problem is that around 90 per cent of his workload is repeat weekly bookings, something he hadn't factored in when he started. 'It is good,' he says, 'because you know where you are going to go each day, but once you are booked in you have got to keep on with that process. If I do take a week off, people will ask when I am going to make up the time. I dread going in the village shop now because I get cornered by people saying, "Well, I'll see you Wednesday, then", and I have to tell them that I haven't got time. That's how bad it has got.'

Even putting his prices up by a third didn't reduce demand for his services. Melvin says: 'It made no difference. One or two people did say, "Ooh, that was quite a jump", but then everybody just said, "Yes, that's fine".'

He adds: 'I do love what I do. I like a nice, tidy garden and everyone is very appreciative of what I do for them. If it looks good, I can go home happy. I never had that in my old job. But I do need to learn how to say no because I can't carry on being quite so busy as this.'

So how do you deal with having too much work?

If it is a one-off occurrence

If it is a temporary, short-term overload, when a stack of projects are unexpectedly bunched together, all needing to be done right now, here are a few ways to get through it:

1. Think smart

If a client has set a deadline of Friday afternoon, check whether they will be looking at the work you have done before Monday morning or not. People in regular nine-to-five jobs often suggest Friday afternoon regardless of whether or not they actually need the project then, simply because it is the end of their working week; but for you, it could make all the difference having a whole weekend to do the job before delivering it first thing Monday morning.

2. Prioritise content gathering

If there are people you need to speak to, information to track down or items you must buy to get your projects done, do that first before businesses and shops close, otherwise you will be stuck.

3. Do some physical exercise to clear your mind

A friend of mine goes for a thirty-minute run when he has a long night of work ahead of him, but if that sounds too onerous, then a quick walk or a few sit-ups and star jumps will work too.

4. Clear your desk

It's amazing how a clear desk or workspace – or an organised list of tasks – can instantly make everything seem less over-whelming. Sweep everything you don't need onto the floor or into a box or a drawer. You can deal with it later. Just make sure you do.

5. Assemble snacks

There is no point in pretending that a couple of carrots and a small pot of hummus will see you through a long evening of hard graft – you need carbs and sugar and lots of them. The diet can wait.

6. Stay calm

You can do this.

If it is a regular occurrence

If you find that you consistently have too much work to do, you will need to make more fundamental changes to the way that you work. You will be no good to anyone, least of all yourself, if you become permanently exhausted and overwhelmed. Here are some suggestions:

1. Stop offering to do everything instantly

Start being realistic about how long projects are actually going to take you to do. If a client asks you when you can deliver some work, don't feel pressured into giving them an earlier date than you feel comfortable with, just because you think it will make them happy. And if the client themselves suggests a deadline that you feel will be impossible to meet, negotiate with them to see if you can agree on a better date.

Ultimately both you and the client want the same thing – for you to do the best possible job that you can within a realistic timeframe – so it is in both your interests to ensure that you have enough time to do it. Just make sure you do all the negotiations at the start of the project – it is not fair to start moving the goalposts halfway through.

2. Analyse the way you work

Are you too slow, inefficient, spending too much time on irrelevant tasks that will make no difference to the end result? Do you waste hours creating a detailed menu, plan or illustration when a rough outline would suffice? Do you spend an hour interviewing people on the phone when ten minutes would do it? Are you always popping out to the shops to buy essential equipment that you should already have in stock? Look carefully at every aspect of your working practice and you may well find plenty of ways to cut down on wasted time and speed up.

3. Increase your fees

The first thing you are taught in economics lessons is that demand falls as the price rises. So if you are able to set your own rates for your work, try it out for yourself and start charging more for your services. You should see a gradual reduction in the amount of work coming your way as you ease out the clients who can no longer afford your fees; if not, that means you were charging far too little in the first place – appreciate the additional income and seek another solution.

If you don't feel comfortable simply hiking your rates up, then introduce different tiers of service – perhaps a higher rate for one-off projects or last-minute requests and a standard rate for repeat work.

4. Swap smaller for bigger

If you have too much work because you are taking on lots of small projects for several different clients, look at ways in which you can switch to doing bigger projects for fewer clients. This will potentially deliver two advantages. If you have fewer clients, you are less likely to have deadline clashes because more of the work is being done for the same person so you can organise a sensible schedule together. If you run three events for the same organisation, for example, they are going to ensure that they are spaced out and are not all held on the same day. Doing bigger projects is also likely to give you more scope to manage your time within it. If you are making a dress for someone, for example, you will be tied to a single deadline, whereas if you are making an entire wardrobe for them, you can create your own schedule around which pieces to make and when.

5. Consider hiring someone to help you

Depending on the type of work you are doing and the agreement you have with the client, it may be possible to get someone else to do some of the more time-consuming and low-skilled elements of the project that will make no difference to the quality of the end result: chopping up onions, for example, or putting email addresses on to a spreadsheet. Of course, you will have to pay your helper for their time, but if it enables you to take on projects that you would otherwise have had to say no to, it might be worth it.

6. Schedule more efficiently

If your work involves travelling to see your customers – perhaps you are a mobile hairdresser or nail technician doing home visits – then look at ways of organising your appointments better, so that you waste less time travelling between jobs. Perhaps you could designate different days for different geographical areas, so that all your appointments on one day are in the same location. In fact, you could use this idea to help you promote your business too: if you announce to potential customers that you will be in their area on certain days, it may prompt them to make a booking.

7. Push for greater predictability

Consider whether you can get your client to schedule the work they give you in a more predictable way. If you often do work for them but they always assign it at the last minute with little notice and short deadlines – making a delivery for them, perhaps, or doing an illustration – see if you can set up an arrangement with them whereby you know you will always be doing this work for them at the same time every month. Not only will you be able to schedule your workload better but by tying your client into an ongoing arrangement, you have also just created your first regular income stream. Congratulations.

8. Invest in up-to-date technology and reliable equipment

Make sure you have equipment that is dependable and reliable – because if it doesn't work, then you can't either, and that could mean having to let clients down if you are not able to complete a job on time. Investing in good-quality equipment that works fast and efficiently – such as a powerful computer, high-spec video camera or advanced kitchen gadget – could save you not only time but also money in the long run if you are not constantly having to pay someone to fix it or to hire a replacement while yours is out of action.

9. Build a support network

If you find that feast or famine is a regular occurrence in your line of work then you need to create a network of useful people you can call on in a crisis. This may be a friend who can pick your child up from school at short notice, or a neighbour who is happy to collect essential parcels from the post office for you, or it might be an industry expert you can rely on to provide the statistics you need, or a picture framer who lives around the corner and works late. Put them on speed dial and let them know how important they are to you.

Remember that it won't be for ever

It may be weeks, it may be months or even years, but one day this overload of work will be gone. So hold on tight when there's too much work, do the best you can and think of the money.

A few years ago, Oliver Webb, who works for himself selling advertising space in medical journals, found himself snowed under. It got so overwhelming that he considered hiring someone to help him: 'There was a point where I had an awful lot of work on and I thought that I probably needed somebody else to help me. But it was going to be incredibly difficult to do that because I would have had to find somebody who had the same kind of reputation that I already had, so that the agencies I work for would trust that this person could provide them with the same level of service that they were getting from me.'

In the end, Oliver didn't hire anyone and simply powered through all the work himself. It turned out to be the right decision: 'For two or three years I was absolutely crazily busy and worked incredibly hard. But I am rather glad that I didn't find anyone because shortly afterwards, there was a shift in the industry away from print into digital, which makes much less money. So I wouldn't have been able to sustain having somebody else working with me anyway.'

TOP TIP

Arrange for recurring bills to be paid automatically by direct debit, so you don't have to remember to deal with them when they are due. When you are in the throes of a work crisis you really don't want to have to start thinking about whether or not you paid your television licence.

Chapter 17

The ten secrets of success

'We are all in the gutter, but some of us are looking at the stars'

Oscar Wilde, playwright

To improve your chances of making a success of working for yourself, try adopting some of the following strategies. These are my ten key steps to the top:

1. Be a diplomat

Every time you are taken on by a new client or customer, you are stepping into the unknown. You are entering their world, and there is so much that you don't yet know – why they want to hire you, how many other people they have tried out before you or what decisions were taken to get them to this point.

So tread carefully and be sure not to offend or upset anyone. Don't gossip and be careful what you say: that DIY disaster you have been hired to fix could have been done by the customer's best friend; that brochure you have been brought in to rewrite could have been originally created by the client; that prestigious event you have been brought in to organise could have been the idea of someone in the team who really wanted to organise it themselves but had it taken off them. Be respectful and professional.

2. Think and act like a business

Regardless of the tax and accounting structure you have chosen for your work, it can be really useful to start thinking and acting like a business. After all, this is not a hobby – it's a serious career which has the potential to support you for many years to come.

That means you should be continually thinking about the issues that other businesses face: how you can improve the services you offer; how you can deliver consistently good customer service; and how you can build your brand.

It also means always behaving in a professional way, being disciplined with your time, delivering consistently high-quality work and, above all, continually thinking about where the next piece of income-generating work or customer is coming from.

3. Don't expect praise

For some reason, clients can sometimes be reluctant to tell freelancers or suppliers how good they are; perhaps because they worry that it might encourage them to increase their fees. This means that if you are working for yourself, you need to be sufficiently self-confident not to crave praise for work you have done, no matter how brilliant it was.

In fact, if you are delivering goods or services remotely, rather than providing a face-to-face service, you should consider yourself lucky if they even thank you for delivering your work – sometimes you will only know that it was acceptable when they pay your invoice. It can be quite dispiriting to work really hard on something for days or even weeks on end and get no kind of acknowledgement in return, but you must see it as a business transaction, as the client clearly does, and focus instead on the money and the freedom that doing the job for them has just given you.

4. Enlist the support of friends and family

Working for yourself is going to be so much easier to achieve if you can do it with the blessing and support of your family and friends, particularly those who live with you. It will make all the difference in the world to know that they have got your back, even during the tough times when clients are being difficult or the job is problematic, your home and social life are constantly being disrupted because of work and your phone is permanently attached to your ear.

Mark Sanders gave up his job as an IT salesperson many years ago to work for himself renovating properties to rent out as holiday homes. He now works from his home in Manchester and is bringing up his two teenage daughters on his own after the death of his partner from cancer. He says: 'My children understand what I do. They see the responsibility of it and the hours I put in, and they are very glad that I am able to work this way. Working for myself means that I have been able to be involved in their lives ever since they were born, and I am pretty much always at home when they get back from school. We probably have more takeaway meals than most people because I have to do bits and pieces of work in the evenings, but I have a phenomenal relationship with them. They know that family life is more important to me than my work.'

5. Be visible

If you are working remotely for clients who find it hard to embrace the idea of giving work to someone they can't see, make a point of popping in to see them every now and then for a catch-up, even if you have to invent reasons to do so. If you are working as a tradesperson, make a regular point of calling or meeting up with the client to explain what you have been working on that day and why. They will love you for it.

6. Don't count your chickens

Don't rely on any work that hasn't been definitively confirmed and nailed down – not just because projects can get derailed at the last moment, but also because time can move at a different speed for a client trying to get approval for budgets and schedules from other people higher up an organisation. Projects that sound like they are all set to go can take months to actually get over the line, as other people get involved in the decision-making, meetings have to be organised and other things get in the way.

When I was given a commission to write opinion pieces for senior managers at a large accountancy firm, it took them four whole months to get back to me to continue a conversation about work we had already agreed to. When the person co-ordinating the project did finally get in touch, long after

I assumed that the project had been abandoned, he simply emailed cheerfully: 'Few days, few months ... who's counting?' Well, I was, actually.

Even if work does look like it is definitely coming your way, people's schedules can also change, so you can't always rely on the start dates you are given for a project. So don't sit around waiting for projects you have been promised to get the green light, because that is a surefire way to go broke. The only income you can really count on is what you have already earned and received. That applies to ongoing work too, which can unexpectedly come to an end simply because a client changed their mind or ran out of money or moved on to a different role: that weekly yoga class you run at a leisure centre, that boardroom lunch you cater for every month – they could crumble to nothing before your eyes, no matter how long you have been doing them for.

On the plus side, other work you had no idea was even on the cards will often unexpectedly pop up out of the blue. So go with the flow, be happy to do the work you have in front of you and don't make important financial decisions based on projects that may never get off the ground.

7. Be prepared to be different

Although a growing number of people are starting to work for themselves in all areas of life, in many situations you may well still find yourself in the minority. And that can sometimes cause confusion, curiosity or even jealousy from the salaried people you are working with. In a world where most people still work regular, fixed hours in a permanent job, week in, week out, they can sometimes feel uncomfortable about working with freelancers and self-employed people who are able to stay at home all day and can choose how and when they work.

If you are working remotely for a small business which is staffed entirely by employees, for example, you need to be prepared to deal with an endless stream of questions about your day. I've had people I am working for start a conversation with anything from 'What are you doing today?' (answer: well, it rather depends on what you are about to say) to 'Ooh, are you outside? Are you somewhere nice? Are those birds I can hear singing?' (Answer: yes, yes and yes, can I help you?) Or they might get a bit funny about the fact that you are not physically sitting at the next desk to them and say things like: 'Is it a bad time to call, because I never quite know when to ring you.' (Answer: please feel free to ring me anytime if you are offering me more work.)

If you provide your services as part of a bigger team made up of permanent employees, then no matter how friendly and welcoming individual people are, they may still treat you differently simply because you are not one of them. As a freelance contractor, for example, you may find that everyone except you is taken out for a celebratory lunch, or is given a Christmas hamper by the management. Or even that everyone except you is invited to a strategy meeting. It can be hard to deal with in the moment; you just have to bite your tongue and remind yourself why you have chosen to work the way you do.

David Perrin has been working as a self-employed IT contractor on and off since 2000. He specialises in providing services in requirements engineering, systems architecture and quality and compliance, particularly for the pharmaceuticals industry. He typically works onsite at a client's office for three to four days per week, on six-month contracts which can often be extended for up to two years.

David says that while he might be physically working with a team, as an independent contractor the rules of engagement are very different and can take some adjusting to: 'Regular staff members will often be involved in discussions and meetings that as a contractor you won't, even though in principle you may have more relevant experience and skills than some of them. This requires a certain fortitude. You can't afford to get offended that the regulars are huddling off to have a strategy meeting, because they have hired you to produce particular deliverables that they can't do themselves due to missing skills or resources, or in some cases to do work which they find dull. Of course, you should offer your expertise, but if these situations bother you, it may be that working this way isn't right for you.'

8. Be open to opportunities

Opportunities for work as a self-employed person can come in all shapes and sizes, and some of them will not be immediately obvious. You may find yourself sitting next to someone at a party who starts talking about how a key member of staff is leaving and the person they have appointed to take over won't be able to start for several months, leaving a gap in the team at a critical point in a project. *Bingo.* Or you may discover through a chance conversation in the supermarket that the local caterer is retiring and now everyone is worried about who will cook for their parties. *Bingo.* Or you might hear that many of the small firms in your area are in a panic because they need to switch to using cloud-based data storage, but they have no idea how to go about it. *Bingo.*

Working for yourself does not come with a set of instructions. It is not like following a recipe in a cookbook, where you know exactly what the outcome will be. It is far more haphazard. It's more like going to the cupboard, picking out a selection of random ingredients you like the look of – your skills, ideas, inspiration – and then seeing what happens if you mix them all together.

And that's what makes it so very exciting.

9. Have something of your own to pour your love into

This is one for people who do creative work. Clients can sometimes be a bit like cute little puppies, happy to simply be hanging out with you and delighted with any attention you give them. Other times they can be demanding, voracious beasts, determined to squeeze every last ounce of creativity and energy from you.

They may take one look at a project you have done for them, then share it freely within their organisation, subjecting it to a dozen conflicting layers of feedback and comments. Then they will come back to you and get you to rip out all the best bits, redo and redesign it, rewrite or reshape it, over and over again, possibly throwing in some other misguided ideas of their own, until the piece of work you are doing for them bears absolutely no resemblance to the original brief.

So if your work involves being creative for other people, it can be really helpful to keep a separate strand of work that is just for you, and you alone – stuff that hasn't been commissioned and may never be sold, but which allows you to be your very best and purest self, untouched by commercial demands, other people's ideas or the need to earn a living.

That way, you can be completely selfless about the work

you do for other people, helping them to realise their vision with confidence and a generous spirit, even if it is not remotely in line with your own, knowing that you will always have your own small corner of creativity where you are completely in charge.

10. Hold on to the fear

There is one thing that will kill a self-employed career stone dead – complacency. If you become complacent, you will stop looking for new opportunities, stop pitching for new work, stop learning new skills, stop taking the time to find better ways of doing things. And then, one day, you will look around and discover that you don't actually have a self-employed career anymore because all your clients have fallen away and you were never bothered enough to find others to replace them. So hold on to the fear that gripped you on the very first day you began working for yourself: the fear of not doing a good-enough job, the fear of not making enough money, the fear of wasting opportunities, the fear of letting people down, the fear of letting yourself down. Not so much fear that it becomes overwhelming but a healthy level of apprehension to keep you on your toes – because that will drive you to keep striving and pitching and achieving, and will ensure that you stay on track to success.

Conclusion

'Never say no to adventures. Always say yes,
otherwise you'll lead a very dull life'

Ian Fleming, author

Deciding to work for yourself can be one of the most exciting, life-affirming decisions you will ever make. Yes, it
can be hard work, especially when you are starting out, and
yes, it can be unpredictable.

But for the sheer thrill of being able to take control of how
and when you work, and for the unbelievable rush of freedom
and joy when you suddenly realise that you are steering this
ship – and that no one else will ever again have the power to
take your career or your work choices away from you – nothing else comes remotely close.

There is one more benefit. That is happiness. Research
suggests that working for yourself can make you a lot happier than being in a salaried job. A report from the Centre
for Research on Self-Employment in 2018 found that people
who have chosen to work for themselves have higher levels of
life satisfaction and wellbeing than employees. Meanwhile a

survey of five thousand workers in the UK, US, New Zealand and Australia, conducted in 2018 by researchers at the universities of Sheffield and Exeter, found that self-employed people are happier, more engaged in their work and experience greater career satisfaction than people in salaried jobs.

So what are you waiting for?

* * *

Whether you are already working for yourself or still deciding whether to make the move, I would be delighted to hear from you. You can contact me via:

Twitter at @rachelbridge100
email at rachel@rachelbridge.com
via my website, www.rachelbridge.com

People mentioned in this book

Lizzie Bett – www.yolkcatering.com

Luis Costa – www.luiscostaphotography.com

Cass Helstrip – www.whitetigerpr.com

Amanda O'Brien – www.theboutiqueadventurer.com

Stoney Parsons – www.stoneyparsons.co.uk

Sarah Jane Moon – www.sarahjanemoon.com

Rachel Mounter – www.mounterfitness.com

Oliver Webb – www.owmedia.co.uk

Phil Lowe – www.phil-lowe.com and www.facetofaceleadership.com

Trevor Merriden – www.merribornmedia.co.uk

Alex Mallinson – www.alexbam.com

Katy Carlisle – www.thewheelexists.com

Mark Sanders – www.hugeholidayhomes.co.uk

Acknowledgements

People who work for themselves are the kind of people who really seize life with both hands and it has been incredibly inspiring and rewarding to have been able to spend so much time meeting and talking to them while writing this book. I would really like to thank everyone mentioned in these pages for so generously sharing their experiences, thoughts and insights. I would also like to thank my agent Robert Dudley and my publisher Zoe Bohm, as well as Jillian Stewart and the rest of the team at Little, Brown, for their help and support. Finally, a big thank-you to my mother Linda and sister Sarah for all their good advice, and an enormous hug to Jack and Harry for making every day amazing.

Rachel Bridge

Index